JUDGE NORBERT EHRENFREUND

and

LAWRENCE TREAT

AN OWL BOOK

HENRY HOLT AND COMPANY

NEW YORK

YOU'RE THE
JURY

SOLVE TWELVE REAL-LIFE COURT CASES
ALONG WITH THE JURIES WHO
DECIDED THEM

Henry Holt and Company, Inc.
Publishers since 1866
115 West 18th Street
New York, New York 10011

Henry Holt® is a registered trademark
of Henry Holt and Company, Inc.

Published in Canada by Fitzhenry & Whiteside Ltd.,
91 Granton Drive, Richmond Hill, Ontario L4B 2N5.

Library of Congress Cataloging-in-Publication Data
Ehrenfreund, Norbert.
You're the jury: solve twelve real-life court cases along with
the juries who decided them / Norbert Ehrenfreund and Lawrence
Treat—1st ed.
"An Owl book."
p.   cm.
1. Jury—United States—Popular works.   2. Instructions to juries—
United States—Popular works.   I. Treat, Lawrence.
II. Title.
KF8972.Z9E35   1992
347.73'752—dc20
[347.307752]   92-6952
                                         CIP

ISBN 0-8050-1951-0

First Edition—1992

ILLUSTRATIONS CONCEIVED BY JULIETTE COSTIGAN
ILLUSTRATED BY CHRIS COSTELLO
DESIGNED BY KATY RIEGEL

Printed in the United States of America
All first editions are printed on acid-free paper.∞

3   5   7   9   10   8   6   4   2

FOR

ROSE AND JULIETTE,

TWO EXTRAORDINARY WOMEN

CONTENTS

ACKNOWLEDGMENTS

The authors would like to thank Theresa Burns, our editor at Henry Holt and Company, for her guidance and courtesy throughout this project; Vicky Bijur, our literary agent, for her expert advice and encouragement; attorneys Nelson Brav and Glen Niemy, who have graciously read and suggested improvements to the manuscript; and to all attorneys and judges who have contributed their notes and memories of cases presented.

INTRODUCTION

Ever been a juror? If not, here's your chance. But even if you have, here's another chance.

Imagine you are sitting in a courtroom. You've just been chosen as a juror after what seemed endless questioning: Have you ever been arrested? Has your wife, your son, your grandfather? Do you have a bumper sticker on your car? If so, what does it say? The questions go on and on. Some seem pointless. Others dig deep and force you to analyze this process of justice. Can you presume the defendant is innocent even though charged with murder, rape, child molestation, and seven other counts? Under our system you must be able to adopt that state of mind and hold to it unless and until the defendant is proven guilty beyond a reasonable doubt—a difficult task, to be sure.

As the judge takes the bench and you look around, you realize you are special. Perhaps it occurs to you that as an American there are basically only two duties you may be required to perform as a citizen—military service and jury service. You become aware of the awesome power you have as a juror in America—to grant millions of dollars in damages, to decide if someone is guilty or not guilty of a crime and, in some states, even the power to decide if another human being should live or die. Once you return a verdict of not guilty, no one can change it, not even the judge. There is no appeal from a not guilty verdict.

It wasn't always so. In fourteenth-century England, juries could be locked up in jail without food or drink until they reached the verdict that satisfied the judge. And if the judge decided the jury reached the *wrong* decision, he could convene a second jury to convict the first jury of returning a false verdict!

Juries existed as far back as two to three thousand years ago in ancient Greece. The first jurors were witnesses who had seen the crime or transaction, but in the course of time the original jurors needed more information, and they called in other witnesses whose credibility had to be examined and weighed. Gradually the jury became the finder of fact that it is today.

The right to trial by jury as we know it originated in England in the year 1215. A group of barons were upset because King John was issuing decrees against them without giving them a voice. The barons, jealous of this violation of their rights, confronted the king in his tent on a meadow called Runnymede along the road to London. They demanded he sign a paper guaranteeing various freedoms including the right to trial by jury. He backed down and signed one of the most important documents in history—the Magna Carta.

Thus began the cherished tradition that America inherited and has struggled to uphold from its very birth. When Thomas Jefferson wrote the Declaration of Independence, he listed as one of the grievances against English rule: "For depriving us, in many cases, of the Benefits of Trial by Jury." And when General Eisenhower spoke to his officers on the eve of D Day in June 1944, he reminded them that one of the freedoms they were fighting for was the right to fair jury trials—a right trampled on by the Nazis.

There are criticisms of trial by jury: it takes too long, it costs too much, jurors cannot understand complex issues, they are too easily swayed by emotions or by sharp lawyers. Such attacks on the system have some validity. But they are outweighed by the fact that the jury trial is still the best protection we have against injustice. It is one of the best examples of democracy in action, representing the judgment of a cross section of the community, not a judge or police officer or government official, but the people. Finally, it has become a marvelous educational tool: every day across the country thousands of Americans pass

Traditional seating of jurors by number in the jury box.

through our courtrooms as jurors, learning about their Constitution and their Bill of Rights, and for a few hours or a few days rising to a new level of responsibility.

In this book certain aspects of a jury trial are missing: there are no long arguments by attorneys; no annoying delays for conferences between the judge and attorneys at side bar or in chambers; no waiting in the hallway for the trial to get started; no deliberations with other jurors who can't understand your point of view. In these twelve cases, *you're the jury.*

Many of these trials raise difficult questions because they go beyond the written law to the heart of one's moral code. Could you, for instance, find a father guilty of kidnapping his twenty-four-year-old daughter from a cult he believed was poisoning her mind? Does a wife who has been repeatedly battered by her husband have the right to kill him out of fear he will beat her again? Which is it, murder or suicide, when a man helps a close friend die in order to avoid the ravages of AIDS?

There are civil trials here too: a daughter's plea to the jury to let her ninety-two-year-old mother die in peace; a woman's suit for one million dollars in damages against her former lover for his intentional infliction of emotional distress. Could you grant their wishes, based on the evidence?

Many jurors are not aware until they sit through their first criminal trial that the prosecution has the only burden of proof—it is the prosecution's job to prove the defendant guilty beyond any reasonable doubt. The defendant is presumed innocent and does not have to do anything, say anything, or prove anything. That is a basic rule in our jury trials, and that is why the prosecution always presents its case first.

Put yourself in the place of one of these twelve jurors as you listen to the details of each case. When the trial is over, turn to the jury instructions in the back of the book; they present the law that applies to each case. What would your verdict be? After you've made up your mind, read through the questions and answers that follow each trial, and finally, read on to see what the real jury decided—and why.

"Ladies and gentlemen of the jury, the case is now in your hands."

YOU'RE THE
JURY

STATE v. CARTWRIGHT

You are juror number one, and District Attorney Alan Weckstein arouses your curiosity in his opening statement when he says that this is the most bizarre murder he ever prosecuted.

"One bullet," he says, and he pauses as his deep-set eyes fix you with a penetrating stare. "One bullet—and it pierced the hearts of two innocent persons, Marlene Ransom and Martin Hogan, and left them dead. We will prove that this man, Roy Cartwright, fired that shot and did so with the premeditated and deliberate intent to kill them both."

Weckstein seems satisfied that he has impressed you in the jury box. He yields the podium to young Donald Ryder, a small, bouncy man who is attorney for the defense.

Ryder is obviously incensed at the D.A.'s attitude, and he states sharply in his opening: "Roy Cartwright never intended any harm. This was an accident, pure and simple. He is a gentle, law-abiding man, and he has already suffered far beyond what most human beings are ever called upon to experience. Roy's grief will burden him for the remainder of his life."

You look at the defendant, who sits motionless, staring straight ahead—a stocky, balding, humorless-looking man in his fifties.

"And why was this accident so tragic?" Ryder continues. "Because that bullet caused the death of Roy's two best friends."

The first witness for the prosecution is a grizzly-looking man in his seventies, Frank Kersey. He testifies he is the caretaker of Family Cottages, a residential complex of about twenty studio cottages where Marlene Ransom had lived for the last seven years. On the morning of July 7, 1989, he was making his rounds when he heard a sharp bang. As he neared the rear of cottage number nine he heard the sound of running water. He went toward the sound and noticed that the water pipe about four feet high behind number nine had sprung a leak and water was pouring out of a hole in the pipe. Then he noticed a hole in the back wall of number nine, about the same height as the pipe. He heard what he thought was a low moan inside the cottage.

"And did you investigate further?" D.A. Weckstein asks.

A: I figured something was up. I knew Marlene was inside, since her car was still there. So I went around to the front.

Q: Tell the jury what you saw.

A: The door was ajar. I called for Marlene, but there was no answer. I peeked in, and . . . oh, my God . . .

Q: Just take it easy and tell us what you saw.

A: It was the most horrible sight. There was Marlene and this guy lying together on the floor in a puddle of blood. I took one look and figured they were dead. I got out of there and called the cops.

Q: You know the defendant, Roy Cartwright?

A: Sure, I seen him around there a lot.

Q: Did you see him there that morning?

A: I seen his car leave earlier. But I didn't think—

Q: That's all, thank you.

Ryder begins his cross-examination politely, almost deferentially.

Q: Have any reason to think Roy here would shoot Marlene?

A: Who? Him? Naah. He loved her. He was tender-like to her. He'd never do anything like that, not unless it was an accident.

Q: You were around number nine many times when Roy was there visiting her?

A: Sure, lots of times.

Q: Ever hear Roy and Marlene argue?

A: Never.

Q: Ever hear Roy act hostile to anyone?

A: No, never.

The next witness is Police Officer Guy Robb, the first officer on the scene. He testifies the first thing he did was to check the pulse and heartbeat of Marlene Ransom and Martin Hogan and found they were both dead. Blood was still coming out of both of their chests. Their bodies lay on the floor together, Hogan's head propped up against the back wall. Both lay on their backs, eyes open; Ransom's body lay partly on top of Hogan's, both still warm to the touch. He turned the bodies over and saw blood oozing from their backs.

He looked about the room for evidence. On the back wall above the bodies, 49 inches from the floor, he noticed a hole that looked like a bullet had passed through the wall. He searched the room for any empty cartridges but found none. On the bed near the front door he found a large piece of wrapping paper from a gun store.

At Weckstein's request, the officer draws a diagram of the scene (see page 4).

Officer Robb further testifies that after the bodies were removed, he searched outside the cottage for the expended bullet or bullets. He still wasn't sure how many shots had been fired. He saw the hole in the water pipe and then saw another hole in the wall of the cottage next door, about ten feet from number nine, also about the same height as the other holes. He went inside the cottage next door after receiving permission from the frightened occupants, and on the floor of the kitchen found what he was looking for—a spent rifle bullet.

The prosecution then calls Emily Masterson. She is a timid woman about thirty years old, and as she raises her hand to take the oath you can tell she is reluctant to testify. When she gets to the witness stand she stops.

"Your Honor, do I have to testify?"

"We just want the truth," the judge says.

"I don't want to testify unless you order me to, Your Honor."

"Then I will have to order it."

Mrs. Masterson testifies she is Cartwright's only child from his former marriage. He had been living with her and her daughter—his granddaughter—at the time of the shooting. She wanted him to end the relationship with Marlene, because she knew Marlene had been unfaithful to him. Yet her father was obsessed with Marlene and insisted he was going

to marry her. On the morning of the shooting she was in the kitchen of her home, about two miles from Family Cottages, when she heard a loud bang and a cry of pain from her father's room. She rushed in to find him lying on his bed holding a rifle in his hands, the muzzle up against his face, one side of his face covered with blood. He couldn't talk, but she realized he had tried to kill himself. She called an ambulance, and he was taken to the hospital. After leaving him at the hospital with the doctor's assurance he was out of danger, she returned home and found a note on his bed.

Weckstein shows her a piece of paper.

Q: Is this the note?

A: Yes.

Q: You recognize the handwriting?

A: Yes, it's Dad's.

Q: Please read it to the jury.

She is close to tears as she reads the note: "Marlene is dead. Please take care of my body."

Mrs. Masterson also identifies the rifle Weckstein shows to her as the rifle she took from her father after he shot himself.

The defense attorney, Ryder, has only a few questions.

Q: You know your father better than anyone. What is his reputation?

Weckstein is on his feet. "Objection, Your Honor! The question is vague. Reputation for what?"

Judge: Sustained.

Ryder: I'll rephrase it, Your Honor. Mrs. Masterson, what is your father's reputation for being a law-abiding citizen?

A: He never was in any trouble in his whole life. Quiet; respects the law. He has a good reputation for being decent in every way.

Q: What is his reputation for being nonviolent, peaceful?

A: He never hurt anyone.

She is about to leave the stand when Weckstein remembers something else. He approaches her with a small envelope and places it on the witness stand before her.

"Would you open that, please."

She takes out a small metal object.

Q: You recognize what that is?

She looks at it and nods her head.

A: Yes, it looks like what I found in my father's pocket after he shot himself.

Weckstein holds it up for all to see.

Q: Looks like an empty cartridge of a bullet, doesn't it?

A: I believe so, yes.

"That is all, thank you."

The next witness is Jason Wilkes, a young clerk from Krane's Gun Shop; he testifies he sold a Mauser 7-millimeter rifle to a man on July 2, 1989. He identifies the same rifle that Mrs. Masterson identified as the one he sold. He also identifies a purchase slip for the rifle of $156.22, taken from his records. He cannot be sure the defendant is the man who bought the rifle, but Roy Cartwright looks similar to the person. He remembers the purchaser was unfamiliar with rifles and had to be shown how to load one. He identifies the wrapping paper that Officer Robb found on the bed as the paper he used to wrap the rifle.

The last witness for the prosecution is Dr. David Featherman, the autopsy surgeon. He examined the bodies for the cause of death and found each died from a bullet wound to the chest and heart.

"Was it the same bullet?" Weckstein asks.

"Objection! Beyond his expertise."

"Sustained," the judge says. "That's for the jury to decide."

But the judge allows the doctor to describe the path and position of the bullet that entered and exited each body, based on his examination of the entry and exit wounds. The doctor testifies that the bullet that killed Marlene Ransom entered her body on a path at a right angle to her body, and the position of the bullet at entry was also perpendicular to her body. The point of entry measured 48 inches from her toes. He draws the diagram below to illustrate:

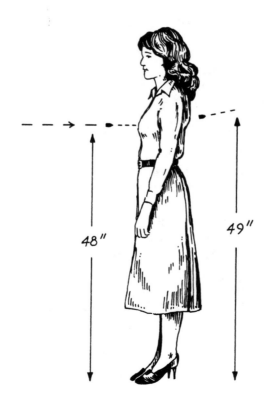

He explains that the bullet exited her back slightly higher than at entry. Upon exiting, the missile changed course because of the obstacles encountered while passing through the body, moving a little upward as well as slightly sideways.

The doctor explains that when the bullet entered Martin Hogan's body, it was not traveling straight as in Ransom's case, but in the same tumbling motion it exhibited when it exited Ransom's back. This tumbling—rolling forward over and over—upon entry into Hogan's chest indicated the bullet had struck something else before reaching this point. Further, the height of her exit wound and his entry wound were almost precisely the same—49 inches.

The bullet continued to tumble as it passed through Hogan's body, and it changed course again as it exited. The doctor illustrates it as shown below.

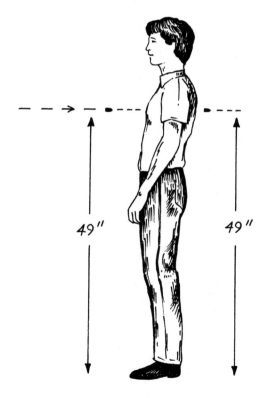

Q: Can you tell us, Doctor, the position of the bodies at the time the shot was fired, that is, how close to each other?

A: I can make a very good guess.

"Objection!"

"Sustained. No guessing here."

Q: Well then, Doctor, can you at least tell us if the two victims were seated or standing, or even lying down, when the shot or shots were fired?

"Objection! He was not there."

"Sustained."

Weckstein sits down, apparently exasperated by the judge's rulings.

"Your witness, Counsel," he says to Ryder, who remains silent for a few seconds before beginning cross-examination.

Q: On the basis of all your training and experience, Doctor, are you able to tell this jury if the shot or shots were fired intentionally or accidentally?

There is a long pause.

A: I cannot say that, no.

Q: Any sign of struggle?

A: None I could observe.

When the doctor leaves the stand, Weckstein announces he has no further witnesses, and the prosecution rests.

Ryder opens the defense case with a number of witnesses who testify to Roy Cartwright's good reputation for two character traits: for being a non-violent, law-abiding citizen, and for being a thoroughly honest gentleman. One such witness is Dale Stearns, manager of The Right Spot, a restaurant where Martin Hogan worked as a short-order cook. Stearns also testifies that Hogan and Cartwright were the best of friends, that Cartwright ate most of his meals at his place, and that he never heard a hostile word between them. Another witness is the Reverend Dudley Haseltine, pastor of the church regularly attended by Cartwright. The minister testifies Cartwright is highly respected by other parishioners. The defendant's granddaughter, Melissa Masterson, age fourteen, testifies along the same lines. No one ever heard Cartwright say a hostile word about Marlene or Marty.

Ryder stands as if to make an announcement. "The defense calls Roy Cartwright."

The defendant walks to the stand slowly, solemnly, shoulders sagging. When the clerk asks him if he swears to tell the truth, he almost shouts "I do!" You can see the scar across the side of his cheek where the bullet went through.

Cartwright testifies he retired from the navy after twenty-four years of service as an aviation chief machinist mate, divorced his wife of many years, then became acquainted with and eventually fell in love with Marlene Ransom, twenty-five years his junior. They started having an intimate relationship while she was still married and living with her husband. One day she asked Cartwright to move into the cottage next to the one she shared with her husband, which he did gladly. After that, whenever her husband beat her up—which was often—she would come over to his place with her eyes black and blue and stay with him a few days, then return to her husband. When her husband left her, Cartwright asked her to marry him. She said she couldn't because she wasn't divorced yet. His grown daughter, Emily, persuaded him to move into her place a few miles away, but he and Marlene continued to see each other quite a bit.

Cartwright says he was in love with Marlene and believed she was in love with him, and it did not make him jealous that she sometimes saw other, younger men. He believed they would marry when she obtained her divorce.

His best friend was Martin Hogan. A few weeks before the shooting he brought Marty over to Marlene's cottage and introduced them to each other. He could tell Marlene liked Marty, but that did not bother Cartwright; he knew she loved him.

He admits that five days before the shooting he bought a Mauser 7-millimeter rifle at Krane's Gun Shop because he had decided to go deer hunting. He put the rifle in the trunk of his car and kept it there. On the morning of July 7, about nine o'clock, he drove over to Marlene's house with some shirts she had promised to iron for him. He also brought in a bottle of Seagram's whiskey, and they both took a nip from time to time while they talked and she ironed the shirts. Then the phone rang and Marlene answered it.

Ryder paces back and forth as he continues direct examination.

Q: Do you remember what Marlene said on the phone?

A: I didn't pay much attention until the very end when I heard her say, "Come on over, Roy's here."

Q: Did you know to whom she was speaking?

A: After she hung up she told me it was Marty who called.

Q: Then did he arrive later?

A: Yes, about fifteen, twenty minutes later.

Q: Did you and Marty greet each other?

A: Sure. Why not?

Q: Then what happened?

A: Marlene offered him a drink, but he said he didn't want a drink until he got off work.

Q: So what did you three talk about?

A: Well, she talked about this nice apartment that Marty and two other bachelors shared together—she had been over there at a party one night recently. She said it was really a nice place, and that when she got some of her bills caught up and a little money ahead, she would get a nice place like that.

Q: Did the subject of the rifle come into the conversation?

A: Not at first.

Q: Later did it?

A: Well, Marlene was telling how bad her place was to live, and she asked Marty to come over to the window so they could look out and she could show what a mess it was in the back.

Q: And did they go over to the window?

A: Yes.

Q: And where were you?

A: I was by the front door, so I said, "I'll show you the gun I bought."

Q: What did she say?

A: She said, "Oh, okay."

Q: Did you have the gun there?

A: No, it was in the trunk of my car.

Q: And where were they when you went out to get the gun?

A: They were still looking out the window by the kitchen.

Cartwright then testifies how he went out to the car, got the rifle, and brought it into the house. It still had the wrapping paper on it, so he stopped at the foot of the bed near the door and was just taking the wrapping paper off when it suddenly discharged.

Q: Did you say anything before the gun fired?

A: I think I said, "Well, here's the gun."

Q: That's all?

A: Yes.

Q: Did you mean for the gun to go off?

A: No, I didn't.

Q: What happened?

A: Well, it hit Marlene and Marty.

He says he stood there for a moment stunned. He looked at them both lying on the floor. The next thing he remembered is going out to the car with the gun, then going back in to look at them again. He didn't know what to do. Then he went back to his car, drove to his daughter's place, and wrote a suicide note to her. He sat on his bed, put the end of the rifle barrel in his mouth, with the butt end between his knees, and pulled the trigger with the intent to kill himself. But somehow the bullet went through his cheek, and he didn't die; he was taken to the hospital, where the doctors treated him, sewed up his cheek, and after a few days released him to the police. Tears fill his eyes when he says he loved Marlene. And Marty was his best friend. He never intended to hurt either one.

Up to this point, the prosecutor, Weckstein, has hardly raised his voice. You have the feeling, however, that soon the fire inside him will flare up.

"You may cross-examine, Mr. Weckstein," the judge says, but Weckstein is bent over in his seat searching through the black briefcase on the floor beside him. You wait while he continues to poke through his case. Finally he finds whatever he is looking for—a small metal object, which he slips under his notebook. You don't find out what it is until later. Now he speaks.

Q: You ever fire a rifle before that morning?

A: Well, I—

Q: Did you?

A: Well, yes, when I just joined the navy. I was on the rifle range at Camp Lewis, Washington. I was just nineteen then.

Q: You were nineteen? So that was, let's see . . . you're fifty-five now . . . that was thirty-six years ago, right?

A: Yes, I guess so.

Q: And you've not fired a rifle since then?

A: No.

Q: Not until you shot and killed Marlene and Marty—

"Objection, Your Honor. He never said he shot them."

Judge: Sustained.

Q: Did you hear that? Your attorney says you didn't say you shot them. Did I misunderstand? Didn't you shoot them?

A: Well, not . . . not really . . . I—

Q: Didn't you shoot and kill them both with your rifle?

"Objection, Your Honor. The prosecutor won't let Mr. Cartwright finish his answer."

Judge: Sustained. Mr. Cartwright, you may finish your answer.

A: Well, no, I didn't really shoot them, not like you make it sound. It was an accident. The gun just went off.

Q: Oh, I see, you had nothing to do with it?

A: Well, yes, I had the gun in my hand. But I didn't mean for it to fire.

Q: It just went off?

A: Yes.

Q: Did you know it was loaded?

A: Well . . . no . . . I forgot.

Q: Who pulled the trigger?

A: Who pulled the trigger? Well . . . I don't know. It went off.

Q: You don't know who pulled the trigger?

A: Well, I don't know how—

Q: Did Marlene pull the trigger?

A: No, sir.

Q: Did Marty pull the trigger?

A: No, sir.

Q: Anyone else in the room?

A: No, sir.

Q: I will ask you again, Mr. Cartwright. It's a very simple question. Please listen to the question: Who pulled the trigger?

A: I presume my hand must have done it.

Q: Was your hand on the trigger?

A: I don't know.

Q: When's deer-hunting season?

A: What?

Q: I said: When is deer-hunting season?

A: Well . . .

Q: You say you bought the rifle to hunt deer, right?

A: Yes, sir.

Q: So, I ask you again: when is deer-hunting season?

A: Well . . . I don't know, sir.

Q: You don't know?

A: But I was going to find out—

Q: You mean you bought this rifle to hunt deer and you have no idea when the season is?

A: Well—

Q: Did you know deer-hunting season was still three months away when you bought the rifle?

A: Well . . . no . . . but, like I say, I was going to find out.

"All right, Mr. Cartwright, I am going to ask you to step down from the witness stand and come over here in front of the jury box and show this jury just how you were holding the rifle when it went off."

"I object, Your Honor," Ryder says. "He has called for a demonstration that cannot be conducted under the same circumstances that existed at the time. It is nothing more than a show-off question—"

"I resent the accusation that I am showing off, Your Honor," Weckstein replies. "I made a very reasonable request. He testified he was holding the gun a certain way when it went off. The jury has a right to see precisely how he was holding it. He is the only one who knows. There are no other witnesses alive."

Judge: Objection overruled.

Cartwright reluctantly steps down from the witness stand and stands in front of you. You notice the beads of sweat on his forehead. Weckstein picks up the rifle. As he walks toward the defendant with it, he informs the court that the rifle has been checked for safety by the bailiff. It is not loaded, the safety lock is on, and there is no possibility it could harm anyone. He hands the rifle to the defendant and asks him to take the position he was in when it went off.

Q: How far was Marlene from you when the gun went off?

A: Oh, about eight or nine feet.

Then Weckstein asks a young woman in the courtroom to come forward.

"Your Honor, this is one of our secretaries. She happens to be the same height as Marlene Ransom. I will ask her to stand at the same distance from the defendant that Marlene was when the gun went off."

He places her about eight feet from Cartwright.

Q: This is how far she was?

"About that, a few inches farther." The woman steps back. "That's it."

"Your Honor, I object!" Ryder shouts.

"Overruled."

This is the scene before you: Cartwright is holding the rifle down around his knees with the barrel pointed upward. The woman is facing him about eight feet away. "Hold that position!" Weckstein shouts, and he pulls out the object he had concealed before. Now you can see it is a steel tape measure. He puts one end of the tape on the rifle and draws it out at the same angle in which it is pointed until it reaches a place on the woman's chest. He turns to the defense attorney.

"Do you stipulate this could be the same spot the bullet entered Marlene's body, Counsel?"

"No, I'll take no part in this circus," Ryder says.

Judge: The record may show the tape has been placed at the same point where the evidence shows the bullet entered Miss Ransom's body.

"Thank you, Your Honor," Weckstein says, turning back to the defendant to continue his cross-examination.

Q: So the line shown by this tape would have been the line of fire, right, Mr. Cartwright?

A: I guess so.

The scene looks like this (see opposite page):

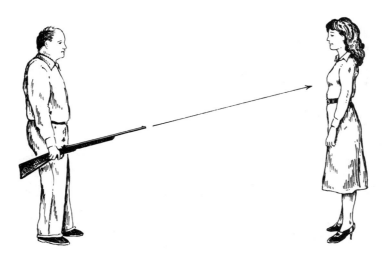

This is how Cartwright claims he was holding the rifle when it fired. The diagram shows what the angle of entry into Ransom's body would have been if the gun had fired in this position.

You can see the line of fire is not a right angle, but about twenty-five degrees below the horizontal.

"Just one moment, please," Weckstein says. He reminds you of a director of a play in rehearsal, instructing the characters what to do onstage.

Now he directs the defendant to hold the rifle at shoulder height, the way he would if he were actually aiming it. Ryder's objection is again overruled. Cartwright does as he is directed, and again Weckstein extends his steel tape from the end of the rifle barrel to the female stand-in, to show how the bullet entered horizontally. Now the scene looks like this (see page 16):

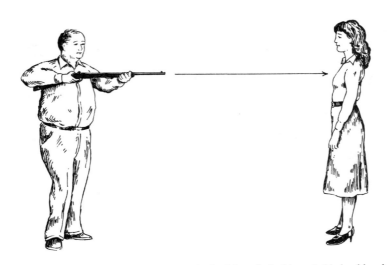

This shows the angle of entry into Ransom's body if the rifle had been held shoulder–height in normal firing position.

Weckstein steps back to allow the picture to sink in.

Q: Isn't it a fact, Mr. Cartwright, that the way you are holding the rifle now, at shoulder height, is the way you held it when it fired?

A: No, no way. Absolutely not!

Q: And that is your testimony, even though the angle of entry from this position, a right angle to the body, is exactly the angle of entry the doctor found in this case?

A: The doctor wasn't there. I was there. I know. As God is my witness, I swear I am not lying. It was an accident. No way did I hold the rifle like this!

Finally Cartwright resumes his seat on the stand. As Weckstein puts the rifle away he asks, "By the way, Mr. Cartwright, this rifle throws out an empty cartridge every time it is fired, right?"

A: That's what I understand, yes.

Q: Do you know what happened to the empty cartridge when you fired the fatal shot?

A: Oh, God, no, I was too shocked to notice that. I loved her so.

Q: I show you this empty cartridge your daughter says she found in your pocket. Do you have any idea how it got there?

A: Well . . .

Q: Well, what?

A: Well, I guess I must have picked it up.

Q: While your two best friends lay dying in front of you, you had the presence of mind to pick it up?

Silence.

———

Possible verdicts as to victim Marlene Ransom:
1. Guilty of first degree murder
2. Guilty of second degree murder
3. Guilty of voluntary manslaughter
4. Guilty of involuntary manslaughter
5. Not guilty

Possible verdicts as to victim Martin Hogan:
1. Guilty of first degree murder
2. Guilty of second degree murder
3. Guilty of voluntary manslaughter
4. Guilty of involuntary manslaughter
5. Not guilty

WHAT ARE YOUR VERDICTS?

[Before choosing your verdicts from each of the lists above, see Jury Instructions 1–3, 5–13, and 16, starting on page 197.]

QUESTIONS AND ANALYSIS

Q1. What was the position of the two victims, Marlene Ransom and Martin Hogan, at the time they were shot?

Q2. What was the most damaging piece of evidence against Cartwright, showing a premeditated and deliberate intent to kill?

Q3. Who did Cartwright intend to kill—Marlene Ransom, or Martin Hogan, or both?

Q4. Cartwright killed two people with one shot. If he intended to kill both he should of course be found guilty of killing both. But suppose that you—as some jurors did—find that he intended to kill only Martin Hogan and killed Marlene Ransom, the woman he loved, by mistake or accident. This could be the case if Cartwright aimed at Hogan and Marlene stepped in front of him at the last second before Cartwright could hold his fire. What would your verdict be then? Would you still find Cartwright guilty of two crimes or only one? Should he be punished for murdering a person he did not intend to kill and to whom he bore no malice?

Q5. What is the significance of Cartwright's picking up the empty cartridge from the floor?

––––––

A1. An attentive jury could figure out the relative position of the two victims when shot. On the basis of the doctor's testimony regarding the entry and exit wounds, the bullet holes in the wall and water pipe were also relevant to this issue. The entry wound to Marlene Ransom's chest showed the bullet entered straight on, at a right angle to her body and without any tumbling motion. This meant the bullet had not yet passed through any other object; it must have struck her first. The entry wound in Hogan's chest, on the other hand, showed the bullet had started to tumble at that point as a result of its passage through her body. How close was she to him? Since the position of the bullet upon exiting her back and entering his chest was the same, and since the height of her exit wound and his entry wound were also the same, it would be reasonable to conclude she was immediately in front of him, her back touching his chest. Were they standing, sitting, or lying down when shot? The bullet hole in the wall behind them and its subsequent path through the water pipe outside showed they must have been standing, because of the line of fire. A likely scenario is that Marlene stepped in front of Martin to prevent Cartwright from shooting him, hoping that Cartwright would never pull the trigger to shoot her.

A2.   Cartwright bought the rifle five days before the shooting and kept it in the trunk of his car. He had no reasonable explanation for buying it. He said he bought it to go deer hunting, but deer season was months away, and he had never hunted deer in his life. The purchase of the rifle was the strongest evidence of a deliberate and premeditated intent to kill one or both of the victims.

A3.   The question of who Roy Cartwright intended to kill was never resolved by the jury. Some jurors believed he intended to kill only Martin out of jealousy but that Marlene stepped in front of Martin at the last moment before Cartwright could stop himself from pulling the trigger. One juror thought Martin stepped behind her to protect himself. Another thought Martin was in the act of embracing her. No one believed it was an accident.

A4.   When a person murders one person and another is accidentally killed by the same act, the law is in conflict as to how many murders he committed. One court's view is that in such a case the intent to kill is transferred by law to the unintended victim, and the defendant should be held equally responsible for both deaths he caused. This is known as the *doctrine of transferred intent*. But other courts say he should be convicted only for the victim he intended to kill; otherwise there would be no difference in penalty between the killer who intends to kill only one and the killer who intends to kill both.

A5.   After firing the fatal shot, Cartwright picked up the empty cartridge from the floor and left with it in his pocket. This act of concealing the evidence was very telling on the issue of deliberation. It certainly was not the normal reaction of a poor soul who had just accidentally shot his two best friends.

VERDICT

GUILTY OF MURDER IN THE SECOND DEGREE
AS TO BOTH VICTIMS

This verdict was apparently a compromise between those jurors who wanted a verdict of murder in the first degree and those who favored a lesser degree of manslaughter. Jurors are not supposed to compromise, but they often do.

(Sentence: Five years to life in prison on both counts.
Sentences to run concurrently.)

STATE v. MAYFIELD

You are juror number two, watching as Deputy District Attorney Miriam Desloup rises slowly to her full height to begin her opening statement. In a strong but emotion-filled voice she says that the defendant, state highway patrol officer Edward Mayfield, stopped young Donna Nugent on the night of December 27, 1989, as she was driving south on Interstate 37.

"Why did he stop her? We don't know. We may never know. But the evidence will show he directed her off the highway to a dark, secluded spot where he strangled her with a rope and threw her body off the bridge.

"When you have heard the evidence," she concludes, "I am sure you will find the defendant guilty of murder in the first degree."

You study the defendant as he listens impassively. He has the good looks of someone who could model for a clothing catalog.

"Circumstantial evidence!" the defense attorney, William Silver, short and feisty with a high-pitched voice, says in his opening statement. "Fibers! Bloodstains! Tire marks! Facial scratches! That's all they have. No eye witnesses. Ladies and gentlemen of the jury"—he looks each of you in the eye—"is it enough? That's what you'll have to decide."

The first witness for the prosecution is the regional commander of the state police. He testifies that on December 27 Mayfield was working the afternoon shift on Interstate 37.

Q: What procedure was Officer Mayfield supposed to follow when stopping a motorist?

A: Our officers are trained to pull the motorist over to a spot that is relatively safe, to keep their conversations with the public to a minimum, and at all times to remain in view of other motorists. In other words, they're supposed to stay on the side of the highway if there is room.

Q: And was there room on Interstate 37 at the Steinmetz exit ramp?

A: Yes, sir. Enough to make a stop right there.

The next witness is Donna Nugent's boyfriend, Clay Garcia. He testifies that Donna was with him at his apartment on December 27. He lives about fifteen miles north of where she lived with her parents. At about 8:00 P.M. she phoned her mother to let her know she was on her way home. She left in her Volkswagen wearing purple pants, a white sweatshirt, and the new white boots Clay had given her for Christmas. At about 10:30 P.M., Clay says, he received a phone call from Donna's mother, who said Donna had not returned home. He immediately set out to look for her in his car.

Donna's brother-in-law, Chris Berkeley, testifies he was among those searching for Donna that night. About 2:00 A.M. he drove down the southbound exit ramp at Steinmetz Road off Interstate 37, where he found Donna's car parked in a cul-de-sac. The passenger door was locked, the keys were still in the ignition, and the driver's window was rolled down. He noticed a dirt road that ran off from one side of the cul-de-sac. He drove down the road to an old bridge but noticed nothing. There was no sign of Donna. He draws a large diagram to help those in the courtroom to understand the scene. He drove to the nearest gas station and called the police.

The first officer on the scene was Alberto Aguirre. He says he searched the area for more than an hour before he found Donna Nugent's dead body in a clump of weeds about sixty-five feet below the old bridge.

Q: Tell us what you observed, Officer.

A: I didn't see any blood. But there were marks—sort of like grooves, reddish marks—on her neck. Several on the left side, one on the right side.

Q: Did they look like rope burns?

"Objection! Beyond his expertise."

"Sustained."

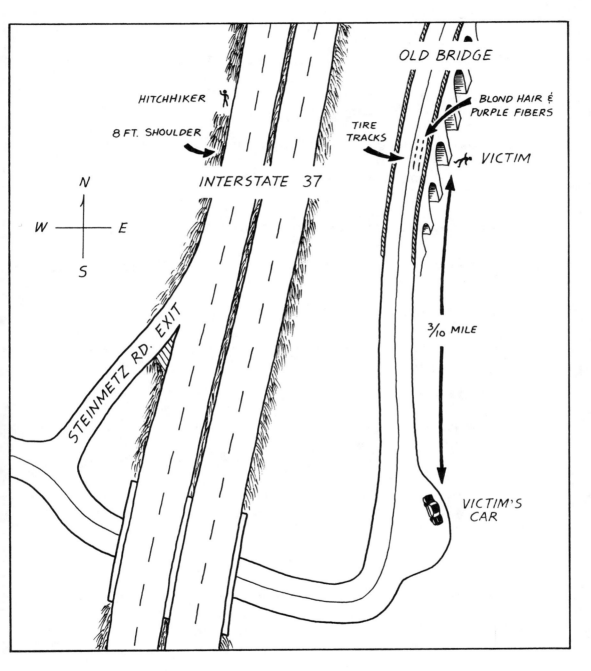

Diagram of the murder scene used by witnesses at the trial.

The county pathologist, Dr. Emmet Turpin, takes the stand. He testifies death was caused by asphyxia due to ligature strangulation.

Q: What do you mean by ligature?

A: I mean an object composed of various cords or strands, such as a rope, as distinguished from a wire.

The D.A. picks up a yellow rope about three feet long from the clerk's exhibit table.

Q: Were the marks on her neck consistent with having been caused by this rope?

A: They were.

On cross-examination, the defense attorney, Silver, shows the rope to the doctor again.

Q: Doctor, are you telling the jury that this rope caused the marks on her neck?

A: No, sir.

Q: You can only say it's possible—might have—is that right?

A: That's true.

As the doctor is leaving the stand, Silver stops him.

Q: By the way, Doctor, did you find any evidence of rape or any other sexual misconduct?

A: I did not, sir.

Officers Joe Petrocine and Richard Sears testify to what they found at the scene. Petrocine found a long blond hair, similar in color to Donna's hair, on the cement railing of the bridge directly above the spot where the body was found. Sears found purple fibers on the same railing, similar in color to her purple pants.

Court adjourns for the day. The judge admonishes you not to discuss the case with anyone and not to let yourself form any opinion about it until it is finally submitted to you for deliberation.

The next morning, the first witness is Carl Waldron, who states that at some time between eight and nine o'clock on the night in question he and his friend Lynn Philips were driving southbound on Interstate 37 when they saw a state police car stopping a light-colored Volkswagen at the Steinmetz Road exit ramp. He saw the emergency lights go on on top of the car. "I remember," he says, "because Lynn turned to me and said, 'She's going to get busted!' "

Defense attorney Silver examines a report in his file, then says, "You were interviewed by the police on January 5?"

A: Yes, sir.

Q: And at that time you said you were not positive what night you saw a state police car stop a Volkswagen. Isn't that correct?

A: I guess so, if it's in the report.

The next witness is Charles Simpson, who says that he and his fiancée Carol Hooks left her parents' residence on the night of December 27 in a rented limousine, which suffered a mechanical breakdown on Interstate 37. The chauffeur managed to drive down the Steinmetz exit ramp, where he parked. Around 9:30 P.M. the chauffeur left to get help.

Simpson testifies that while he was waiting in the limousine he saw a police car, traveling fast, come from under the overpass of Interstate 37 and go up the south entry ramp.

Mayfield's daily activity log for December 27 is now introduced as evidence. It shows that at 9:20 P.M. Mayfield wrote a traffic ticket to one Stephen Northcutt. A document expert testifies that the entry was originally written as 10:20 P.M. but was subsequently scratched out and touched up to read 9:20.

The log also shows that between 9:30 and 10:00 P.M. Mayfield bought gas from a Shell gas station near Marymount Boulevard and Interstate 37.

Alice Wentz takes the stand and says she works at the same Shell station. She was working there the night of December 27 when around ten o'clock a state police officer came in for gas.

Q: Will you describe what you saw when he came in?

A: Well, he had some scratch marks on his face. He seemed very nervous, and he looked disheveled.

Q: Do you see that person in the courtroom?

A: I do.

She points to the defendant. "That's him."

The next witness, Mary Knox, is also a gas station employee who was working when Mayfield drove in to get gas. She states, "While Alice was filling his tank, he was standing by the trunk of his car wiping down various objects, like he was trying to clean things."

Q: Just what did he do?

A: He wiped down something that looked like a flashlight, except I couldn't see it too clear, and then he wiped off his nightstick.

Q: Then what?

A: Well, when he went to sign his credit card, he had claw marks on the side of his face, only it looked like he was trying to hide them.

Q: How could he hide them?

A: By cupping his nose with his right hand, only he had to take his hand away when he bent down to sign the card, so I said to him, "You must have had a bad night." He kind of looked at me like he didn't understand, and then he said, "Bad? I've had one hell of a night."

A series of state police officers then testify as to events on the night of December 27.

At about 10:25, Officer Salomino Amiel saw Mayfield in the parking lot near state police headquarters. Amiel saw three large vertical scratches on the right side of Mayfield's face.

Two other highway patrol officers came on duty at ten o'clock to work the graveyard shift. They made a preshift check of the car Mayfield had used. They said the trunk was somewhat disarrayed, the car was not in its normally clean condition, and they did not see a rope in the trunk at that time.

At about ten-thirty, Sergeant Robert Mallone spoke with Mayfield. Sergeant Mallone said Mayfield had an "open, bleeding wound" on the back of his right hand; Mayfield's face was "red and puffy-looking," and there were noticeable welts.

Janet Coates, a city police officer, states she was patrolling in the vicinity of Interstate 37 on December 31 when she was directed to go to the Steinmetz Road area to meet a state highway patrol officer who was detaining possible murder suspects in the Nugent case. Coates spoke there to Mayfield, who said the suspects had been riding their motorbike in the Steinmetz Road area. Mayfield said he had detained them because "you know the crook always returns to the scene of the crime."

Officer Coates testifies that Mayfield was very curious about the Nugent murder investigation by the city police. He wanted to know "details" about it. When she explained to him what could be learned from skin samples, she noticed him cleaning his fingernails. Coates felt Mayfield was pressing her to tell him what the homicide investigators thought had "really happened down there." When she told him someone had taken Nugent to the old bridge and thrown her off the west side, Mayfield motioned to the east side of the bridge and said, "She wasn't thrown over there, she was put over here."

Mayfield asked Coates what she thought would happen to the person who committed the crime if caught. Coates said, "I hope they die a slow and painful death." Coates testifies Mayfield got angry with her, saying, "You don't know what you're talking about . . . it could have been something that got out of hand, it could have been something that just went too far."

The following day is devoted to expert testimony on the physical evidence.

Albert Lackner, an expert in fibers, testifies he compared a single gold thread found on Donna's sweatshirt with the threads on the shoulder patch of the defendant's uniform.

Q: Did you form an opinion as to those threads?

A: Yes. I concluded they had the same microscopic characteristics, and therefore the fiber from the shirt could have come from the shoulder patch.

Q: Did you find any distinction whatsoever between the thread on the shirt and the threads from the patch?

A: None whatsoever.

He also says that fibers found in Donna's hands were similar to fibers from the patch, and that purple fibers found on Mayfield's gun and boot could have come from Donna's purple pants.

A serologist, an expert in the identification of body fluids, testifies he analyzed a bloodstain found on the victim's boot and compared it to the blood of the victim and the blood of the defendant.

Q: What blood type was found on the boot?

A: ABO blood Group A, Estrase D1 and PGM1.

Q: And the blood type of Donna Nugent, what type was that?

A: Her blood type is ABO Group O, Estrase D1 and PGM 2-1.

Q: What is Edward Mayfield's blood type?

A: His blood type was ABO Group A, Estrase D1 and PGM1.

Q: And from that analysis you were able to conclude that the bloodstain found on that boot could not have come from Ms. Nugent but could have come from Officer Mayfield; is that right?

A: That's correct.

Defense attorney Silver looks up from a document he is studying and starts his cross-examination.

Q: Mr. Lackner, what percentage of the population has the blood type found on the boot?

A: About 18 percent of the general population.

Q: Okay, so what you are saying is that about 18 percent of the population has that type, and that Officer Mayfield is among millions of people who have that type?

A: Yes, sir.

Q: It is not like a fingerprint, which you could say definitely came from him?

A: Correct.

The witness gives similar testimony with regard to bloodstains on Donna's shirt: they could have come from the defendant; they could not have come from Donna.

An accident investigator testifies he examined fresh tire tracks on the bridge near the railing where the blond hair and the purple fibers were found. He measured the distance between the tracks. He also measured the distance between the back tires of the Chevrolet police car Mayfield was driving that night. The distance was the same.

Upon cross-examination, defense attorney Silver brings out the fact that none of the expert testimony identifies Mayfield specifically.

The prosecution's final witness is another state officer, who testifies that on January 6, ten days after the murder, Mayfield's patrol car was searched again. This time a yellow rope, about three feet long—the same one counsel used in examining the pathologist—was found in the trunk.

Q: Is that rope standard issue equipment?

A: It is not, sir.

Silver is brief on cross-examination.

Q: Do you know why it was not found before, when the trunk was searched?

A: I don't know, sir.

The prosecution rests. D.A. Desloup offers her exhibits in evidence, and they are received without argument.

———

Silver opens the defense case by calling a number of character witnesses, who attest to Mayfield's excellent reputation as a law-abiding citizen.

A fingerprint expert from the police department testifies none of the fingerprints found in Donna's Volkswagen belonged to Mayfield.

Mayfield's daughter, Sandra, testifies she has a purple jacket made by Mayfield's wife, who did her sewing in the living room of their home; that while the sewing was going on, the purple cloth for the jacket was usually kept on the living room couch; and it was Mayfield's habit on coming home after work to put his gun and gun belt down on this same couch.

The defense calls its own expert on fibers, who testifies that the purple fibers found on the defendant's gun and boot could have come either from his daughter's purple jacket or the cloth on the couch. He also says the fibers from Mayfield's shoulder patch can be distinguished from the fibers found on Donna's shirt and hands.

Marcia Davis, a serious-looking woman wearing no makeup, takes the stand. She testifies that on the evening of December 27 she was driving her car southbound on Interstate 37 between seven-thirty and eight and was passing the Steinmetz Road exit.

Q: Did anything unusual take place?

A: Yes. I was approaching the Steinmetz exit when I saw a man standing at the side of the highway, apparently a hitchhiker—

D.A. Desloup interrupts, "Objection, Your Honor! Irrelevant. Whether she saw a hitchhiker has absolutely nothing to do with this case."

The Judge replies, "Overruled. I will hear the evidence, subject to a motion to strike." To the witness he says, "You may proceed."

A: He was apparently a hitchhiker, because he was waving his arms as if he wanted me to stop. Then he lunged out as if to get in my way to make me stop. I said to myself, "This guy must be crazy—"

"Objection, Your Honor. What she said to herself is irrelevant."

"Sustained."

The D.A.: Motion to strike, Your Honor.

"Motion granted. The jury will disregard the last statement as to what the witness said to herself. Proceed."

A: Well, anyway, I had to swerve in order to avoid hitting him. He was waving his arms in a crazy way.

Q: Can you describe him?

A: I was so upset and it happened so fast, all I remember is that he was a man.

D.A.: I move to strike the testimony, Your Honor. It's irrelevant. It's guesswork.

Judge: Overruled. It's for the jury to decide.

Silver looks pleased with the judge's ruling. He calls three other motorists, who give similar testimony. One of the witnesses, Albert Sandoz, adds that the man was "waving money and jumping in front of cars," apparently in an effort to make them stop.

As his final witness, Silver calls one of Mayfield's fellow officers, John Bannister, who says he saw scratches on Mayfield's face the night of December 27 at about ten o'clock.

Q: Did you ask him how he got the scratches?

A: I did.

Q: And what was his reply?

A: He said he was chasing a suspect and fell against a barbed wire fence and scratched his face.

D.A. Desloup cross-examines:

Q: Did he tell you where this happened?

A: No.

Q: Did he tell you if he caught the suspect?

A: He said the guy got away.

The defense rests. Mayfield does not take the stand.

"Any rebuttal by the prosecution?" the judge asks.

The D.A. clears her throat. "Your Honor," she says, "I realize it is still early on this Friday afternoon. I need the weekend to prepare my rebuttal. May we adjourn until Monday?"

The judge grants her request and sends the jury home for the weekend, reminding you not to discuss the case with anyone.

On Monday morning the D.A. begins by calling Irma Pollard. She is in her early twenties, blond and attractive. She testifies that a month before the murder she was stopped by Officer Mayfield while driving south alone on Interstate 37 at night. He directed her down the Steinmetz exit ramp and asked her to get out of her car. He told her she'd been driving too slowly. After a brief conversation about her family, he let her go.

Silver jumps to his feet.

"Objection, Your Honor. In the first place, it's irrelevant. Just because he stopped this lady there doesn't mean he did the same with Donna Nugent. In the second place, it's improper rebuttal. The D.A.'s been lying in the weeds with this—"

"That's enough, Counsel!" the judge interrupts him. "We'll discuss it at side bar, out of the hearing of the jury."

The attorneys go to the side of the bench, and there is a furious exchange of whispers you are not supposed to hear. You can't help but hear some of the words, however. You hear Silver say "highly inflammatory" and the judge say, "truth is what we want," but the rest is unclear. Finally the attorneys return to their places. Silver is visibly upset.

"Proceed, Counsel," the judge says. "Objection is overruled."

The witness is still on the stand. The District Attorney resumes.

Q: Miss Pollard, tell the jury how you came to be a witness in this trial.

A: I was watching TV last week, and I saw the news about this case. It sounded familiar, so I called your office.

Silver takes a deep breath and squares his shoulders before beginning cross-examination.

Q: Did he tell you why he directed you off the highway?

A: Yes. He said it was safer. Too dangerous on the highway with all the drunk drivers these days.

Q: Didn't touch you?

A: No.

Q: Didn't do anything out of line?

A: No. He was very polite.

There follows a string of eighteen witnesses. Most are women in their twenties who testify they were driving alone on I-37 when stopped by Mayfield and directed down the same exit ramp for some minor violation. Nearly all say they contacted the D.A.'s office within the past few days after seeing news of the trial on television, too late to testify in the prosecution's case-in-chief. Only two were not driving alone, one of whom had

three small children asleep in the backseat and another whose husband
was slumped down in the passenger seat. Under cross-examination all
admit the defendant acted courteously at all times and never made any
sexual advances.

"Let the record show my objection is a continuing one for all these witnesses," the defense attorney says.

"So noted," replies the judge.

One witness is a young man named David Bloom. He has long blond
hair, which hangs down well over his shoulders. Bloom testifies that on
the night of December 2, 1989, he was driving alone on Interstate 37
when Mayfield ordered him to pull off the highway and go down the
Steinmetz exit ramp.

D.A.: At the time of this stop, was your hair the same as it is now?

A: A little longer.

Q: Was it blond then also?

A: Oh, yes.

Q: Was it dark at the bottom of the exit ramp?

A: Real dark.

Q: What happened when the defendant came up to your car?

A: He looked at me in surprise. He said, "Oh, my goodness" when he
saw me. I think he thought I was a girl—

"Objection, Your Honor! What the witness thought is not relevant."

"Sustained."

"Motion to strike—"

"Granted. Ladies and gentlemen," the judge says to you, "the last statement of the witness as to what he thought is stricken from the record. Disregard it."

D.A.: What did he say?

A: At first he seemed too confused to say anything. Then he mentioned something about my headlight, that it looked out of alignment.

Q: Was it?

A: No, in fact I'd just had my headlights checked a few weeks before.

Q: Then what?

A: He let me go.

Denise Carrier, an attractive woman in her twenties, is called as the
state's final witness. She testifies that on December 15, while driving south

on Interstate 37, she was pulled over by a state police car. It was about 10:30 P.M. The officer told her over his loudspeaker to drive all the way down the Steinmetz exit ramp. She got out of her car and he got out of his, and they met between their two cars. It was dark and cold. He said her headlight was too low or too high, she couldn't remember which. He noticed she was cold, and he asked her to get into his car so they could discuss it. They sat in the car for about thirty minutes talking about various things, mostly about her boyfriend. Then he said he would show her the old bridge down the road.

Q: Did you object?

A: I was too scared. I was shaking so that I could hardly talk.

The officer drove about fifty yards to the bridge, where they got out and looked down.

Q: Did he touch you?

A: No, he was very polite.

She says the officer took her back to her car and told her she could go.

"Did he ever give you a ticket?"

"No."

"What happened after you drove off?"

"I was too nervous to drive. I had to pull over and stop for a while so I could calm down."

"Do you see that officer in the courtroom?"

She points to the defendant. "That's him. I'll never forget him."

———

Possible verdicts:
1.   Guilty of first degree murder
2.   Guilty of second degree murder
3.   Not guilty

WHAT IS YOUR VERDICT?

[Before choosing your verdict, see Jury Instructions 1–12, starting on page 197.]

QUESTIONS AND ANALYSIS

Q1. Of all the circumstantial evidence presented by the prosecution, which was the most devastating to the defendant?

Q2. If you were the defense attorney, how could you use the evidence of Mayfield's habit of directing young females off the highway to your advantage?

Q3. The defense attorney made a crucial decision to keep his client off the stand. Was that a mistake?

Q4. Does the fact that this case is based primarily on circumstantial evidence make it a bad case for the prosecution?

———

A1. The defendant's strange habit of directing so many young female motorists off the highway to the same dark, lonely spot where the murder occurred was especially damning to his case. The highly distinctive nature of this evidence pointed to Mayfield as the one who led Donna Nugent to the same place he had lured others.

A2. Faced with such devastating evidence, the ingenious defense attorney used the evidence to his advantage—or tried to. He argued such conduct was really in Mayfield's favor, because not one of the women said he behaved discourteously; not one complained of any improper touching or suggestions of sexual misconduct; he was polite at all times. Such evidence really went to show Mayfield could not have been the murderer, because it was obviously not within his character to be violent or hostile to women.

34

A3.   One of the most critical decisions for any criminal defense attorney in a jury trial is whether to put his client on the stand. Here the jury was anxious to hear Mayfield explain why he stopped all those young women at the same place, how he got the scratches on his face. Of course, the jurors were told they could not draw any negative inference from the fact that he did not testify and were not to permit it to enter into their deliberations in any way. But could you realistically follow such an instruction? Could you keep yourself from thinking, "What's he hiding?" We will never know why Mayfield did not testify, nor whether it was a strategic mistake not to do so. That decision remains a secret between Mayfield and his attorney. But from what we do know it seems he would have made a poor witness. He tended to give himself away several times, when he blurted out on which side of the bridge the victim had been thrown and when he defended the killer to another officer. Moreover, the cross-examiner would have had a field day getting him to explain why he stopped so many women. Better by far to have this young, handsome officer, a family man with a clean record, sit there near his wife and children, and to let the jury wonder how such a person could have done something so terrible. He may also have confessed guilt to his lawyer, making it ethically impossible for him to be called as a witness to deny guilt.

A4.   This case was based almost entirely on circumstantial evidence. There was no direct evidence Mayfield committed a murder; no positive identification; no one saw him at the scene that night; no confessions or admissions were recorded. Does that make it a bad case for the prosecution?

    The answer is no. Of course, some jurors will say they can't convict on circumstantial evidence alone. Prosecutors must be wary of them in jury selection. However, most jurors *like* circumstantial evidence; they are challenged by it and enjoy being detectives. The judge instructs jury members that facts don't *have* to be proved by direct evidence; both direct and circumstantial evidence are entitled to the same weight, and both are equally acceptable means of proof. In fact, circumstantial evidence is often the strongest. A fingerprint, for example, is really only circumstantial evidence, but it is the best proof a person was present at a certain location even though no one saw him. It is often better evidence than direct eyewitness identification, which could be a mistake or a lie. And when the circumstantial evidence points to only one reasonable interpretation—as it did here—jurors feel a special satisfaction in returning a guilty verdict.

VERDICT

GUILTY OF MURDER IN THE FIRST DEGREE

Edward Mayfield was tried twice for the murder of Donna Nugent. Our case includes the evidence at the first trial, which resulted in a hung jury. In the second trial the testimony concerning the hitchhiker and Mayfield's hearsay explanation of how he got the scratches were excluded as inadmissible evidence. In the second trial a different jury convicted Mayfield of first degree murder. The state did not seek the death penalty, although it was within its discretion to do so.

(Sentence: Twenty-five years to life in prison)

STATE v. WASHBURN

You are juror number three, and your eyes fasten on the seemingly inoffensive little man who is the defendant in this case, Tyrone Washburn. A popular junior high school teacher, he is charged with the murder of his wife, Elena.

Washburn's defense lawyer has the look of a County Cork Irishman, with a ruddy complexion and a fine mop of white hair. You've heard of this guy. He used to be the D.A., in fact, but rumor has it he started drinking too much at lunch. In the courtroom one afternoon he challenged a judge who had ruled against him to come down off the bench and fight. So much for his career as D.A. Now when the judge introduces him to you and the other jurors, he just stands and says, "O'Connor's my name."

At the other end of the counsel table, closest to you, sits the prosecutor, Madeline Smith, an attractive woman in her thirties, nearly six feet tall, with a full mane of tawny hair. She seems to dominate the courtroom with her unusual height. "We will prove," she says in her opening statement, "that on the morning of March 12, 1979, Tyrone Washburn cold-bloodedly strangled his wife in the living room of their home while their two children waited outside in the car to be driven to school."

There is a long pause. The judge is looking at Mr. O'Connor, waiting for him to give his opening statement. Finally the old defense attorney shuffles to his feet.

"As Your Honor knows," he says, "the opening statement is not evidence. The evidence will come from the witness stand. We will waive opening statement and let the evidence speak for itself."

The first witness called by the prosecution is Officer Dale Chambers, investigator for the homicide bureau. He testifies he was called to the Washburn residence at 1:45 A.M. on March 13 and found the defendant waiting for him at the front door. Washburn told him he had just discovered his wife's dead body and led the officer to the garage. There Chambers observed the body of the decedent lying on her stomach on the concrete floor in a small pool of blood. She appeared to have bled profusely from the nose. Next to the body was a trash can tipped over on its side. Beside the can were several lamb chop bones, an empty milk carton, and an empty doughnut bag. She was fully dressed, with a gold chain, which was broken, still partly around her neck. A trail of blood in the garage led to the body. Chambers noticed a ligature mark about her neck.

Deputy District Attorney Smith continues her direct examination.

Q: Did you draw any conclusions as to how that mark occurred?

A: Yes, sir, by some object that had been wrapped around her neck.

Q: Such as the gold chain that she had on her chest?

A: Yes, sir—I mean, yes ma'am.

Officer Chambers testifies that the body was cold to the touch. From his sixteen years experience on the force, he believed she had been dead for some time. She had bloody wounds on her hands. He then proceeded to inspect the house. He draws a diagram showing the position of the body in the garage (see opposite page).

Q: Did you find any sign of ransacking?

A: No, sir.

Q: Any sign of forcible entry through doors or windows?

A: I examined all the locking mechanisms, all the doors and windows. In my opinion there was no evidence of any forced entry.

The house was dusted for fingerprints, but they didn't turn up anything. They were all of the Washburn family and the maid. While Officer Chambers was critiquing the case with the other officers of the investigation team in the living room, one of them noticed a wet spot on the carpet. Detective Marsha Dykes reached down and touched it, brought her finger up, and saw that it was blood. It was hard to see, because the color of the carpet was similar to the color of the blood.

Q: Did you do anything as a result?

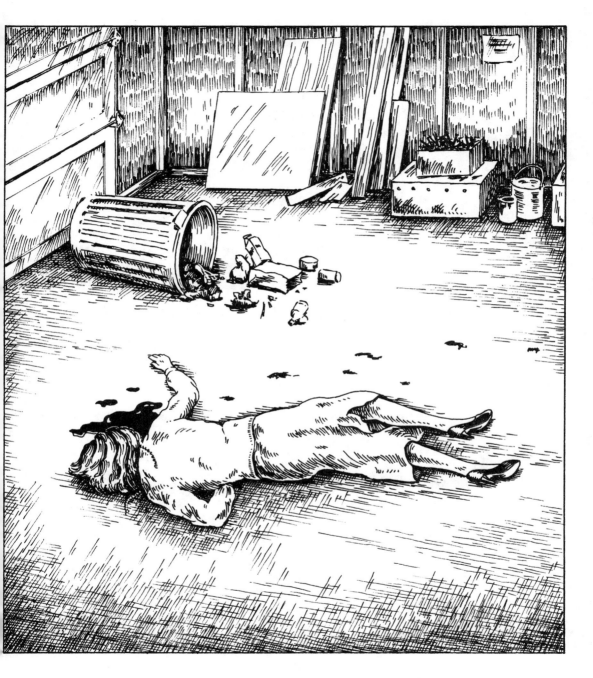

Police sketch showing the position of the body in the garage upon discovery.

A: Yes, sir. We called the evidence technician and asked him to test for blood.

Q: How did he do that?

A: Well, it was getting light, and you need complete darkness to do the test he uses, so we came back the next night. He sprayed the living room carpet with luminol. It's a luminous spray, and when it comes in contact with blood it illuminates, same as what phosphorus does at night.

Q: What happened?

A: To my surprise the whole living room illuminated with this bright phosphorescent color.

Officer Chambers testifies that they sprayed further throughout the house and discovered a bloody trail from the living room through the kitchen to the garage. One of the officers found a wet mop in the kitchen closet, so they sprayed that also, and it lit up with the same phosphorescence.

Q: Notice anything special about the kitchen floor?

A: Yes. From the tests it looked like someone had tried to mop up the blood.

Q: Did it look like an inside job?

"Objection!"

"Sustained."

O'Connor begins his cross-examination. But first he walks over to the clerk and picks up the necklace that has been marked as an exhibit.

Q: This the necklace you found on the body?

A: Yes, sir.

Q: And you think she was strangled with this little necklace?

A: That's my opinion.

O'Connor hands the necklace to the officer on the stand.

Q: Here, take it in both hands. See how strong it is. Go ahead. Just give it a light tug.

The officer hesitates.

"Go ahead. Try it."

"Objection, Your Honor!"

But before the judge can rule on the objection, the officer pulls the necklace apart with one pull. He looks surprised.

Q: Easy to break, wasn't it?

A: I guess so.

Q: Want to change your mind, Officer, about that necklace being strong enough to strangle a woman to death?

A: Well . . .

Q: Do you?

A: I could be wrong on that, yes, sir.

"Thank you, that's all."

A police criminologist, Pat O'Malley, testifies he inspected Tyrone Washburn's body the day after his wife's body was discovered, but could find no scratch marks or blood.

Next the D.A. calls the county coroner, Dr. Kiro Yoshino. He performed the autopsy on Elena Washburn. Dr. Yoshino testifies that in his opinion Elena died of strangulation by an object pressed around her neck. The markings on her body indicated she had been dragged after her death. He found no defensive wounds that would indicate she had been in a struggle. There was no evidence of a sexual attack.

Now the D.A.'s questions focus on the time of death.

Q: Did you form a conclusion as to the time of death?

A: Yes. In my opinion she was killed before breakfast the day before she was found.

Q: Your reasons for that opinion?

A: There was practically no food in her stomach. That means she had not eaten that day.

Q: Any other basis for your opinion?

A: Yes. The police investigator told me she was very cold to his touch when he found her. In his opinion she had been dead for many hours.

"Objection. Hearsay."

"Overruled. An expert may use hearsay to form an opinion."

Q: One more thing. She was found lying on her stomach. Do you have an opinion as to when she was placed in that position?

A: Yes. She had been lying on her back for several hours before being turned over.

Q: How can you say that?

A: Lividity.

Q: What?

A: The process of lividity. When a person dies and lies in a certain position, the blood tends to congest at the lowest spot. This leaves a large bluish discoloration.

Q: And did you find such a spot on the decedent?

A: I did: on her back, indicating she'd been on her back for several hours. Later she was turned over on her stomach, as she was found.

O'Connor begins his cross-examination by attacking the testimony as to time of death.

Q: You say you relied on the officer's opinion as to time of death?

A: Partly, yes.

Q: Did that officer have any medical training?

A: I assume—

Q: Do you know?

A: No, I'm afraid not.

O'Connor goes back to the clerk's desk and picks up the necklace again.

Q: In your opinion how was she strangled, that is, with what instrument?

A: Some sort of garrote.

Q: Some sort of what?

A: A garrote—a cord or wire used for strangling.

Q: Was she strangled with this necklace?

A: Not in my opinion. It's not strong enough.

The prosecution calls Detective Marsha Dykes as the next witness. She testifies she interviewed Washburn at his home on the morning after the body was found. He was not under arrest and was cooperative in every respect. Washburn told her he and Elena had been married twelve years and had two children, Maria, age nine, and Morgan, seven. They had a good relationship. He had no idea who would want to kill her. On the morning of March 12, 1979, he and Elena had a light breakfast together. She had orange juice and toast. He and the children went out to his VW and got in the car. It was his habit to take the children to school every morning on his way to work. Elena had her own car, a van, which she would drive to her job as a county social worker. When he got in the car with the children he remembered a report he needed, which was still in the house, so he went back to look for it while the children waited in the car.

Q: Did he tell you how long he was in the house while the children waited outside?

A: Yes, he said it was only a few minutes—not more than ten or so. He couldn't find it right away.

Q: Did he tell you if he saw Elena in the house then?

A: Yes. He said she was still in the kitchen doing the dishes. It was about 7:45. He kissed her good-bye and drove off with the children. He said he never saw her alive again.

Washburn carefully described to Detective Dykes where he'd been that day—classes all morning with a half-hour break in the middle of the morning, meetings in the afternoon. He came home about 5:00 P.M. and saw Elena's van in the driveway but didn't see her when he went inside. The children were not home either, so he called the sitter, who usually picked them up from school and took care of them until Elena came by to take them home. The children were still at the sitter's. Elena had not picked them up. So Washburn went to get the children and brought them home. When Elena didn't appear for dinner he searched the house for her but did not look in the garage. Her sack lunch was still on the kitchen table, her car keys on the living room couch. He fried lamb chops for dinner and also served the children doughnuts and milk.

Q: Did he say what he did with the lamb chop bones and the other trash?

A: I asked him that and he said he put the bones, and the doughnut bag and the milk carton, in the trash basket in the kitchen.

Q: Did you ask him if he emptied the trash in the garage later that evening?

A: I did.

Q: His answer?

A: He said he did. Right after dinner.

The detective further testifies that Washburn got very worried as it grew later. Finally after midnight he decided to look in the garage, and that's when he found his wife.

Q: Did you ever talk to him again?

A: Yes, two days later he phoned me. He said he wanted to correct one thing in his statement. He then told me he remembers now he did not empty the trash in the garage.

O'Connor on cross-examination:

Q: Did you check out his alibis?

A: I did, and they all checked out for the most part.

Q: As far as you could tell he told you the truth?

A: Yes.

Q: Did you arrest him?

A: No, not then.

Q: When did you arrest him?

The detective checks her report. "We finally arrested him April 12, 1980."

Q: More than a year later?

A: Yes.

Q: Why did you wait so long?

A: We wanted to be sure. We wanted a thorough investigation. After all, he had a good reputation. We wanted to check out all possible suspects.

Q: Find any?

A: No.

Q: So that was why you arrested him—because you couldn't find any other suspects?

"Objection."

"Overruled. You may answer."

The detective glares at O'Connor. "Counselor, we arrested him because we had the evidence."

The next witness is Washburn's neighbor, Jim Martin. He testifies that on the morning of March 12 he saw Washburn driving down the street. He remembers the time, about ten o'clock. He remembers Washburn was going toward his (Washburn's) house. Martin said he was chatting with another neighbor, Oscar Ramirez, at the time.

O'Connor's brow is knitted as he begins his cross-examination.

Q: Mr. Martin, I am confused. Didn't you testify before the grand jury in this case that you were not sure of the date, and not sure what time this happened?

A: That is true, sir. I didn't remember then.

Q: What made you change your testimony?

A: The police had me hypnotized last night to jog my memory. Now I remember.

Q: Hypnotized?

A: That's right, sir.

O'Connor turns to the judge. "Your Honor, I object to this testimony. There are scientific studies to show a witness may not tell the truth under hypnosis. Testimony is not trustworthy if it has been brought on by hypnosis. I move the testimony of this witness be stricken and the jury admonished to disregard it."

The judge ponders this motion for a moment, then says, "Objection overruled. Please proceed."

O'Connor grimaces but goes on.

Q: How can you be so sure it was March 12?

A: Because that was the day I prepared my tax returns. I brought them in to my accountant after lunch, and he told me he'd have them ready the next day. So I went back the next day, signed them in his office, and mailed them on that day. That's why I'm sure.

The D.A. calls her final witness, Ray Deems. He testifies he is a private investigator for the All-Safe Insurance Company, which held a $2,500 policy on the life of Elena Washburn, with Tyrone Washburn as the beneficiary. Deems says his company wanted to find out if Washburn had killed Elena, because if he did, he would not be entitled to the money. About two months after the murder, Deems interviewed Washburn at his home.

D.A. Madeline Smith pauses noticeably before her next question.

Q: What did he say?

A: At first, nothing different from the police reports.

Q: Then what?

A: Then he said something I didn't expect.

Q: What was that?

Smith looks at the jury as if to make sure you are listening.

A: Mr. Washburn said, "I didn't look in the garage because I knew she was in there all the time."

The D.A. lets the answer sink in before she sits down. You hear a buzz of conversation from the audience. "You may inquire, Mr. O'Connor," she says politely.

O'Connor stares at Deems before beginning cross-examination.

Q: Were those his exact words?

A: Something like that.

Q: You took notes?

A: Didn't have to. [Deems points to his head.] It's all up here.

Q: Is it up there word for word?

A: Not word for word, no.

Q: You can't tell us verbatim?

A: No.

Q: Could he have said, "I didn't look in the garage because I was afraid she might be in there"?

A: I don't think so.

Q: Is it possible he said it that way?

A: Anything's possible. But that's not how I remember it.

Q: And this interview was over a year ago?

A: Yes.

Q: You knew this was a very important statement?

A: Yes.

Q: And how long after he said this did you report it to the police?

A: Don't know. Didn't keep track.

Q: Three months?

There is a pause. Deems doesn't answer.

Q: Three months, Mr. Deems?

A: Well . . . yeah . . . about that.

Q: So it wasn't important enough to report for three months?

A: Well . . .

O'Connor just waits.

A: Well, he said something like that. That's all I can say.

O'Connor is finished. The prosecution rests.

O'Connor opens the defense case by calling Elena's sister, Rosa Aguirre. She knew the couple for fifteen years. The family was very close. Tyrone was a loving husband and father.

Q: Tell the jury his reputation for being a peaceful, nonviolent person.

A: Very good. He never once harmed my sister. He'd never dream of striking her. That wasn't like him. They loved each other . . .

She starts to cry. "I just know Tyrone never did this—
"Objection, Your Honor, that's for the jury to decide."
"Sustained. Just answer the question, madam, thank you."

Other witnesses also testify to Washburn's reputation as a peaceful, law-abiding person. The principal of Washburn's school testifies he has known the Washburns for years, and they had a loving relationship.

A minister of the Unitarian church, the Reverend Guy Walton, testifies he attended a meeting with Washburn on the afternoon of March 12, during which Washburn did not appear nervous or upset about anything. He was his usual self.

Three witnesses testify they saw Elena alive during the day of March 12. A neighbor, Perla Francisco, says she saw Elena standing in the front doorway as Washburn and the children drove off in the morning. Another neighbor, Sara Mardikian, says she was looking out her window around noon waiting for her daughter to come home from school when she noticed Elena's van pull into the driveway. She also noticed the van leave about a half hour later.

The D.A. cross-examines:

Q: Was she driving?

A: I guess so. She always does.

"Objection, Your Honor," the D.A. says. "She's guessing."

"Objection sustained," the judge replies. "Please do not guess, madam."

"Move to strike the last answer as to who was driving," the D.A. says, "and I ask the court to admonish the jury to disregard it."

"Motion granted," the judge says. He turns to you. "Ladies and gentlemen of the jury, the last answer as to whether Elena Washburn was driving the car is stricken from the record. You will disregard it and treat it as though you never heard it. Proceed."

A: Well, I don't actually remember seeing the driver, but it was definitely her car.

Christina Ashcraft, a social worker who shares an office with Elena, testifies she saw her for a few minutes in the office in the early afternoon.

All the witnesses complain it is hard to remember exactly because it's been so long ago.

Oscar Ramirez takes the stand. He testifies he was the one talking to Jim Martin in the morning when Washburn's car drove by. He can't recall the exact date, just that it was around March 12. However, he remembers the time being about seven thirty and not ten o'clock as testified to by Martin.

Finally O'Connor calls back Jim Martin as his last witness.

Q: Mr. Martin, you recall you told this jury that you were able to remember you saw my client driving his VW toward his house on March 12 because you filed your tax return the next day, March 13?

A: That's right, sir.

Q: Mr. Martin, I show you this document marked exhibit number eight. You recognize it?

Martin looks surprised. "Where did you get this?"

Q: Please answer the question.

A: Wait a minute! How did you get hold of this? You have no right to this.

Q: Your Honor, would you please direct the witness to answer?

Judge: You may answer, sir.

A: It's my tax return for last year, but how—

Q: Tell the jury what date you wrote down as the filing date.

A: March 15.

Q: Not March 13?

"No, sir." Martin looks confused. "I guess not."

The defense rests.

———

Possible verdicts:

1. Guilty of first degree murder
2. Guilty of second degree murder
3. Not guilty

WHAT IS YOUR VERDICT?

[Before choosing your verdict, see Jury Instructions 1–3, 5–11, starting on page 197.]

QUESTIONS AND ANALYSIS

Q1. What important aspect of a crime, although not a necessary element, was lacking in the prosecution's case?

Q2. What is the significance of finding the trash from dinner (lamb chop bones, etc.) next to the body?

Q3. What is the significance of finding all the doors and windows locked?

Q4. Do you think it was fair for the judge to allow the testimony of the neighbor, Jim Martin, after he had been hypnotized by the police to jog his memory?

Q5. Why do you think O'Connor did not put his client on the stand?

Q6. Why did the prosecution want to show that the necklace was the murder weapon?

Q7. Did the D.A. make a mistake by prosecuting solely on the theory that the victim was murdered before 8:00 A.M.?

Q8. An opening statement is customarily made by both attorneys at the beginning of trial. Why would an old fox like O'Connor choose to waive it?

––––––

A1. The prosecution's case lacked proof of any motive for Washburn to kill his wife. Although motive is not an element of the crime and does not have to be shown, the defense could argue that the absence of motive was a circumstance tending to show Washburn was not guilty. He was a nonviolent, family-oriented husband and father who apparently loved Elena and their children. There was no reason shown by the prosecution why such a man would want to destroy his family.

A2.   The trash found near the body was important evidence because Washburn initially told police he fried lamb chops for dinner and soon afterward emptied the trash (lamb chop bones, doughnut bag, and milk carton) into the trash can in the garage. If he did so, he certainly would have seen the body at that time, not after midnight as he told the detective. This would show he was lying as to when he found the body. The prosecutor could argue that he changed his original story about emptying the trash because he realized how damaging it was—a strong argument for conviction.

A3.   The significance of the locked doors and windows is that it reduces the possibility of a forced entry by a burglar or other strange intruder. It enhances the D.A.'s argument that the crime was an inside job.

A4.   At the time of this trial, 1979, testimony that resulted from the use of hypnosis by the police to jog the witness's memory was generally allowed. Under the law existing then, the judge's ruling to admit Jim Martin's testimony was not considered unfair. Since then, however, the law has changed. Scholarly studies have led the courts to conclude that persons under hypnosis are likely to experience false memories; the subject tends to respond in the way he believes the hypnotist desires, and he is unable to distinguish his true memories from pseudo memories. If O'Connor made his objection to the evidence today (1992), it would be sustained, and Jim Martin would not be allowed to testify.

A5.   The main reason O'Connor did not put Washburn on the stand was because through other witnesses he was able to put everything before the jury that Washburn would have said, i.e., what he told the detective who interviewed him as well as the testimony of those who praised his character and supported his alibi. So O'Connor got what he wanted in evidence without subjecting his client to rigorous and possibly damaging cross-examination.

A6. The prosecution would liked to have shown it was Elena's own necklace that was used to kill her, because that too would indicate an inside job. But no murder weapon capable of strangulation was ever found. O'Connor's effective cross-examination of the investigator regarding the weakness of the necklace opened the way for him to argue the murder weapon had to have been brought in from the outside, then removed.

A7. The D.A. tried this case on the sole theory that the murder occurred at breakfast time while the children waited outside in the car. The coroner's opinion as to time of death, the presence of Elena's sack lunch still in the kitchen, her car keys on the couch—all supported that argument. But reliance on this theory alone turned out to be a mistake in strategy. It placed the D.A. in an untenable position when defense witnesses testified they saw Elena alive that day. If the D.A. had not limited herself to this theory, she might have argued Washburn also had the chance to commit the murder when he came home about five o'clock. As it was, she was locked in.

A8. The purpose of the opening statement is to give jurors a bird's-eye view of what the evidence will be. Sometimes a defense attorney will defer his opening until the beginning of the defense case. In rare cases it may be waived altogether if he or she is not sure what the evidence will show, whether certain witnesses will testify, or, if they do, what they will say. In such situations it may be wiser not to give any opening statement at all rather than risk losing credibility with the jury because the evidence turns out to be different from what the attorney said it would be. You can be sure O'Connor knew exactly what he was doing when he waived it.

VERDICT

NOT GUILTY

There were simply too many unanswered questions for the jury to be convinced beyond a reasonable doubt. Why would Washburn want to kill Elena in the first place? How could the prosecution's sole theory—that the murder occurred at breakfast time—hold up when so many witnesses testified they saw her alive that day? Why did the police take so long to arrest him? In light of these lingering questions, the jury could not come to a decision to convict.

STATE v.
STORM AND MCCLURE

You are juror number four, and you wonder if you can convict a father of kidnapping his own daughter. But that is the charge, and you promised the grim-faced district attorney, John Harmon, that you would hear the evidence and be fair to the state.

Two defendants are on trial. One is Dr. Paul Storm, a prominent surgeon in your community. He is charged with kidnapping his twenty-four-year-old daughter, Joan, in order to remove her from membership in the Church of The Master. Dr. Storm, a distinguished, heavyset man, seems devastated by this strange situation. The codefendant is George McClure, whose name you recognize since he is known nationally for his work as a cult deprogrammer. You are still not sure what that means, but you will find out soon enough. He is also charged with kidnapping Joan Storm but, unlike Dr. Storm, looks unperturbed. Squeezed between the two defendants at counsel table sits Peter Freitag, the attorney for the defense—a nattily dressed fellow with an impeccably clipped mustache.

When Joan Storm takes the stand as the first witness for the prosecution, she doesn't look at her father. She turns and stares at the wall above the jury. She looks quiet, studious, blinks nervously.

"Why are you looking at the wall?" the D.A., Mr. Harmon, asks.

A: Because I don't want to look at him.

Q: You mean your father, Dr. Storm?

A: Yes.

Q: Do you love your father?

A: I love my father.

Dr. Storm starts to get up and move toward her. "Oh, Joan," he murmurs, "please . . ." But his attorney restrains him.

"I love my father," Joan shouts. Already she is crying, her face bent over in her hands. "But I hate what he did to me!"

"Are you ready, Miss Storm?" the judge asks.

She nods, sits up, and under the D.A.'s quiet, direct examination, the story begins to unfold.

In 1987, at the time of this incident, she was living with her mother, Martha Storm, and her eighteen-year-old brother, Jim. Her mother and father had been divorced for six years when he married his secretary, Arlene. Her father and his new wife lived in the same city. In 1985 Joan joined the Church of The Master and became a full-time student of the Church, but she continued to live at home. Ever since his marriage to Arlene, Joan had regularly visited her father and often had dinner with him and her stepmother. She had always been a quiet, rather withdrawn girl, dominated by her father. Dr. Storm opposed her membership in the Church of The Master and often tried to persuade her to give it up, but she was not deterred. Nevertheless the dinners at his home continued. The nature of their discussions changed, however. Joan began standing up to her father, would talk back to him, and would not back down as she had in the past whenever they had an argument. Her stepmother, Arlene, also tried to talk her out of being in the Church. Then one weekend when she came to Dr. Storm's house for dinner, they told her they were going to a surprise party for a friend of Arlene's. They all got in her father's Cadillac and drove about fifteen miles north of town, to a house where she'd never been before. When they went inside they brought her into a room where there were two strong-looking women and George McClure, who was arranging a large TV screen for video showing.

Harmon continues the questioning.

Q: Did Mr. McClure say anything?

A: Right away he started making insults against the Church of The Master.

Q: What did he say?

A: He said it was an evil cult, that I was a mindless idiot for associating with it.

Q: Did you respond?

A: I was shocked.

Q: What did you do?

A: I said, "I don't have to stand here and listen to this, I'm going."

Q: Did you try to leave?

A: I tried to go out through the doorway, but the two women grabbed me and dragged me into the bedroom. I tried to get away. I screamed and yelled. I fought with them, but they held me down on the bed, the two of them on top of me. I was scared . . .

She starts to cry again. The judge hands her a box of tissues.

Q: Can you go on?

A: Yes.

Q: What did you say to them?

A: I said, "Why are you doing this to me?"

Q: Did they tell you why?

A: They said I was a mindless robot, that George McClure was here to deprogram me.

Q: Had you ever heard that term "deprogram" before?

A: I heard it once on the Lou Grant TV show. There was an episode about it.

Q: What did you understand it to mean?

A: They were assuming I had been programmed by the Church, and they were going to deprogram me.

Q: What happened next?

A: One of the women, Madge, yelled into the next room, "Are you ready for her yet?" and Mr. McClure said, "Yes, bring her in."

Q: Did they take you into the film room?

A: Yes, they sat me down under two big camera lights. My father was there, too. So was Arlene. George McClure sat next to me. He had a microphone in his hand.

Q: What did he say?

A: He kept saying I was a mindless robot, over and over again, that I didn't know right from wrong, and that my father had hired him to stay with me until I could think straight.

Q: What did your father do?

A: He was crying. I asked my father, "Why are you doing this to me?"

Q: What did he say?

A: He said, "I'm protecting my investment."

Q: Did he say anything else?

A: I tried to talk to him. I pleaded with him to help me, to let me go, but he just shook his head. Mr. McClure told him not to answer me, and he didn't. He just said, "I'm protecting my investment."

Q: How long did you remain in this room?

A: All day and all night until I went to bed.

Q: What did they do?

A: They kept calling me names like robot; they kept saying I was a vegetable who couldn't think, that I was a zombie.

Miss Storm tells how she was kept in the same house for five days doing the same thing. Sometimes McClure and the two women would lecture her; sometimes they showed her videos of other cults. The two women, Madge and Carla, guarded her all the time. When she went to the bathroom they would go in with her. When she went to bed, one slept beside her while the other slept in front of the door, which was barricaded. She was never left alone. After a week with no change in her attitude they seemed exasperated.

Q: What did Mr. McClure do?

A: He would shake me and say, "Why are you being so difficult?"

Q: What else happened at these sessions?

A: McClure and Madge and Carla and Arlene would all gather round me. They would start yelling at me and calling me these names, circling around me. Then McClure would read to me from some article criticizing the Church, then they would yell again. I was a nervous wreck.

Miss Storm testifies that after a week of frustration they brought in a new woman to help with the deprogramming. Her name was Anna Pettengill. She was a former member of the Church of The Master who had defected after several years and then started writing negative articles about the experience.

Q: What happened with Miss Pettengill?

A: She was supposed to be an expert on the Church of The Master and tried to counsel me. But she didn't approve of Mr. McClure's methods of holding me prisoner, and we became friends. She said she would help me get free. She slept with me, and one night under the covers I wrote down my mother's phone number on a piece of cardboard. She whispered she'd call my mother and let her know where I was. We had to be very careful that Carla, who was sleeping by the door, wouldn't hear us.

Q: What happened to Miss Pettengill?

A: They fired her the next day because they felt she was too sympathetic, and she left.

Q: Did they ever suspect she was going to seek help for you?

A: They must have suspected something, because the next day they packed up and drove me to a new house several miles away. I couldn't tell where it was, because they blindfolded me on the way during the drive over there.

Q: And did the same things happen at the new place?

A: Yes.

Q: Did you see your father there?

A: Oh, yes. He would come in from time to time and ask Mr. McClure how it was going. He still didn't talk to me, because Mr. McClure asked him not to.

Q: Did you ever find a way to be released?

A: I decided to fake it. I told them I was convinced that they were right. I wouldn't go back to the Church if they would let me go. So my father and Mr. McClure said they would let me go if I signed a general release form saying I was there of my own free will and that they hadn't done anything wrong.

Q: And did you sign such a statement?

A: Yes. They drove me to the office of our family attorney, Marvin Felder.

Q: Did you mean it?

A: No. I just did it to get free, and that's what happened. They let me go.

Q: And are you still a member of the Church of The Master?

A: Yes. A full-time student.

The D.A.: Your witness.

When the defense attorney, Peter Freitag, rises to begin his cross-examination, Dr. Storm stops him and whispers something in his ear. Freitag nods reassuringly and pats the doctor on the shoulder.

Q: When you had dinner with your father and stepmother before this incident, did you tell them about the Church?

A: Sometimes.

Q: Did you ever tell them your church taught you to "exteriorize" yourself?

"Objection. Irrelevant."

"Overruled."

A: Yes.

Q: What does "exteriorize" mean?

A: To be able to perceive as a spiritual being.

Q: Did you tell them it meant you could get out of your own body and walk beside yourself?

A: Not quite like that, no.

Q: Something like that?

A: Yes.

Q: What else did you say?

A: I said I was not just a body, but I had a soul, too.

Q: Did you tell them you could see auras of light emanating from your brother, Jimmy?

A: Yes.

Q: And did they seem concerned?

A: Yes.

Q: They were concerned for your mental health, right?

A: Yes, but—

Q: And didn't your father tell you he loved you and wanted to save you from destroying yourself?

A: Yes. He was worried about me.

Q: And he tried to get you to read articles about the Church, didn't he, hoping it would open your mind to the truth?

A: Yes.

Q: Did you read them?

A: No.

Q: Why not?

A: Because I didn't believe them. I could see for myself what the truth was.

Q: Did your father tell you specifically why he didn't want you in the Church of The Master?

D.A.: Objection. Irrelevant.

Judge: Sustained.

Freitag: But Your Honor, are you denying us the right to show why Dr. Storm opposed his daughter's association with this cult?

Judge: Counsel, the benefits or detriments of that organization are not at issue. We are here to decide one thing only—whether the defendants kidnapped this woman. Nothing else.

Defense counsel asks to approach the bench, and there is a heated discussion at benchside between the attorneys and the judge that you cannot hear. When they come back, Mr. Freitag looks as if he lost the argument. Finally cross-examination resumes.

Q: What did your father mean when he said he was protecting his investment?

A: He always saw everything in terms of money. I'm sure he meant he had spent a lot of money on me, and he didn't want to see it wasted.

Freitag picks up a paper from the clerk's desk and walks to the witness stand.

Q: I show you a document marked exhibit five. Recognize it?

A: Yes.

Q: Is that your signature at the bottom?

A: Yes.

Q: You read it carefully before you signed it?

A: Yes.

Q: So you knew exactly what you were signing?

A: Yes.

Q: You knew it could be used in a court of law?

A: Well, I'm not a lawyer, but—

Q: In fact you signed it under penalty of perjury?

A: That's what it says.

Q: You're not in the habit of signing false declarations, are you?

A: No.

Q: This is the document you referred to in your direct examination?

A: Yes.

Q: Are you telling this jury that what you said in this paper was not true?

A: Yes.

Q: You lied under penalty of perjury?

A: Yes, but I only did it to—

Q: Please answer the question! Did you lie under penalty of perjury?

A: Yes, I had to.

Q: So you committed perjury?

A: Yes.

Freitag: Your Honor, I move this document, exhibit five, into evidence and ask that it be viewed by each juror at this time.

Judge: Motion granted. Exhibit five received in evidence. May be passed to the jury.

The paper is passed to the jury. You read it to yourself. It says:

GENERAL RELEASE

I, Joan Storm, hereby declare that beginning September 21, 1987, my father, Paul Storm, M.D., and my stepmother, Arlene Storm, together with others acting on their behalf, attempted to and did deprogram me from my beliefs in the Church of The Master. I believe their actions were justified, that I was not acting with my own free will when I was involved with the Church, and now believe the Church was a cult and in fact brainwashed me.

NOW THEREFORE, I hereby release all claims or causes of action, civil or criminal, I may have had against my father and all others acting in his behalf. I further acknowledge that I have not suffered any mental or physical harm by reason of this deprogramming although I first thought I might. I now realize all actions taken by my father and stepmother and George McClure were for my own good and it is now my intention to disassociate myself from the Church of The Master. I further assert my father committed no crime to my knowledge in attempting to deprogram me. I went with him of my own free will.

I declare under penalty of perjury the foregoing is true and correct.

Executed October 8, 1987
Signed: [Joan Storm]

When the jurors finish reading the exhibit, the defense attorney turns back to Miss Storm.

Q: Isn't it true you left the house on at least two occasions the second week of your stay to go shopping?

A: Under guard, yes.

Q: With Madge and Carla?

A: Yes.

Q: Where did you go?

A: Nordstrom's department store.

Q: Did you request to go?

A: Yes, I needed cosmetics, underwear. Arlene brought me clothes but I needed personal things.

Q: And they granted your request?

A: Under strict guard, yes.

Q: And you went to various counters and made purchases in the store?

A: Yes.

Q: And you talked to clerks?

A: Yes. I bought things.

Q: Did you ever ask any of them for help?

A: No.

Q: Ever cry out for help? Ever say, "Help me, I'm being held prisoner"—Anything like that?

A: No, I was too frightened.

Q: Ever make any attempt at all to escape?

A: No, I couldn't.

Q: Why not? You weren't handcuffed, were you?

A: No, but . . . well, I was afraid to.

Q: Afraid of what? You were among all those people in the store who would have helped you, isn't that true?

A: Yes, but . . . I was afraid no one would believe me, and if I didn't make it, Mr. McClure and his staff would do worse things to me. I'd had enough mental abuse.

Q: The truth is, you could have run away if you wanted to, right?

A: No. Besides, I had no money. Where would I go?

Q: The truth is, you really were there of your own free will, right?

A: No, that's not the truth. I was held prisoner!

Q: The truth is, your mother put you up to making this charge, didn't she?

A: Absolutely not.

Q: Doesn't your mother hate your father?

A: Yes, but what's that got to do with it?

Q: Didn't you talk to your mother about it after you got home?

A: Of course.

Q: And didn't she encourage you to go to the D.A.?

A: It was my idea.

Q: After talking to her?

A: Well—

Q: Please answer my question.

"Objection, Your Honor, he's badgering the witness."

"Sustained. Give the witness a chance to answer, Mr. Freitag."

Q: [quietly now] I will give you all the time you need, Miss Storm. Please answer the question. Did you go to the D.A. after talking to your mother about it? You may answer yes or no.

A: [a long pause] Yes.

Q: And she did suggest it, didn't she?

Joan Storm is on the verge of tears.

A: [another pause] Yes.

Freitag: Thank you, no further questions.

She is crying again as she steps down. She slumps down in the back next to her mother. She is sobbing noticeably as she buries her head in her mother's shoulder.

Now Jimmy Storm, Joan's teenage brother, is called as a witness. His straight blond hair reaches down to his shoulders. You notice his father shake his head disapprovingly as Jimmy takes the stand. He testifies that when Joan didn't show up at home, Jimmy phoned his father to find out where she was. His father replied, "I'm saving her life. She's a zombie and I'm going to have her deprogrammed."

Anna Pettengill is called to testify as to her role in the deprogramming. She corroborates Joan Storm's testimony as to what happened while she was there.

Q: Why did they call you?

A: They said they had a stupid girl who was acting very stubborn. They wanted me to work with her.

Q: Was she stupid?

A: No.

Q: What happened?

A: I told them right away I didn't believe in any restraints. But they held her prisoner. Mr. McClure was very forceful, and he tried to split her from her mother.

Q: What did he say about her mother?

A: He said her mother was evil because she allowed her to be in the Church, and as long as Joan stayed in it she was evil, too.

Miss Pettengill testifies that after a few days McClure asked her to leave because she was too easy on Joan. He wanted her to be more aggressive. She describes how she and Joan hid under the covers so Joan could pass her a note without the guard's noticing. Since she didn't have any paper or pencil, she used a piece of cardboard from her pantyhose and a lipstick to write Joan's mother's number. As soon as she got away she called Joan's mother to tell her where Joan was. She didn't know they would move Joan the next day.

It is time to adjourn. When you go home that night, you do not turn on the TV news or read the local section of the paper for fear you might see something about the case.

On the second morning of the trial, the D.A. announces he has one final witness, Dr. Saul Cordero. Dr. Cordero claims he is a psychiatrist who has testified as to state of mind in many cases. He says he examined Joan Storm and gave her psychological testing. He has reviewed the police reports and read the transcript of Joan Storm's testimony on the stand.

Q: Are you familiar, Doctor, with that portion of Miss Storm's testimony regarding her visits to the department store during her captivity?

A: I have reviewed it, yes.

Q: I refer to those times in which it appears she had an opportunity to cry for help or even escape but failed to do so. Remember that?

A: Yes.

Q: Do you have an opinion, based on your training and experience, why she did not do so?

Freitag is on his feet. "Objection, Your Honor, beyond the scope of his expertise. They tried to use this same kind of evidence in the Patty Hearst case as to why she didn't try to escape from her captors, but the judge wouldn't allow it. It's too farfetched."

"Objection overruled. The doctor may respond."

A: Joan Storm's behavior can be medically explained. It is perfectly understandable. She was suffering from what is popularly known as "Stockholm Syndrome," a name that comes from a case in which a group of hostages in Stockholm became totally under the control of their captors to the point they no longer wished to escape. Here Joan had been imprisoned for several weeks. They watched her every move—sleeping with her, even going to the bathroom with her. It was all a tremendous shock to her. As a result, she lost the power to make decisions. In my opinion she lost the will and initiative to seek help, and that is why she didn't do so.

D.A.: Your witness.

Freitag wastes no time getting to the point.

Q: You examined Joan Storm eight months after the incident, right?

A: Yes, about that.

Q: And you mean to tell this jury you can read her mind and tell us what she was thinking eight months before?

A: I can try.

Q: You can try. Are you a mind reader?

A: I wouldn't call it that.

Freitag: No further questions.

Dr. Cordero is excused, and the prosecution rests.

The defense begins its case by calling the lawyer Marvin Felder. He testifies he is Joan Storm's attorney, that she came into the office with her father and stepmother one afternoon in October 1987 and asked to speak with him alone. Dr. Storm and Arlene Storm waited outside. Miss Storm told him she'd been away for several weeks with her father and others acting in his behalf in a deprogramming session, and now wished to sign a document in that regard.

Freitag: You are aware of course of the attorney-client privilege?

A: I am.

Q: You realize of course that as Joan Storm's attorney she has the right to exercise that privilege and prevent you from disclosing any part of that conversation?

A: I am very aware of that. Yes. And so is she.

Q: And has she authorized you to speak by waiving the attorney-client privilege?

A: She has. As to that conversation relating to the general release only. Nothing else.

Freitag shows the witness exhibit number five, the general release.

Q: You saw her sign this?

A: I did.

Q: She signed it of her own free will?

A: She said so then.

Q: She knew what she was doing?

A: Yes.

Freitag: Your witness.

D.A.: Did she say anything else about this document?

A: Not at that time.

Q: At any other time?

A: I am not authorized to say.

Q: She ever tell you whether she'd been kidnapped?

A: I am not authorized to say.

The defense rests without calling either defendant to the stand. The D.A. goes back to talk with Joan Storm, still seated in the last row with her mother. Then the D.A. announces he has no rebuttal.

The attorneys begin their closing arguments. The D.A. cautions you not to let your sympathy for the father-daughter relationship keep you from doing your duty to follow the law.

Freitag counters by holding up the general release. He has it blown up on a screen so you can read it easily. "She swears in this document that Dr. Storm and George McClure did nothing wrong. Under penalty of perjury. Read it for yourselves—"

Suddenly a voice from the back of the courtroom calls out: "One moment please, Your Honor." It is Joan Storm, standing up. She walks forward to the D.A. and whispers in his ear. He looks surprised. He turns to the judge. "Your Honor, a new development. Evidence has just come to my attention of which I was not previously aware."

"Objection, Your Honor," Freitag shouts. "The testimony is finished. It's too late."

A hubbub ensues between the two attorneys, and the judge calls a recess. When you return you see Marvin Felder already seated on the stand.

D.A.: Recall Marvin Felder.

Freitag: Let the record show the defense objects strenuously to this procedure. It is highly improper, unheard of—

Judge: Your objection is noted, Mr. Freitag. Proceed, Mr. District Attorney.

D.A.: Mr. Felder, do you have new evidence to disclose to the jury?

A: I do.

Q: Why did you wait until now to reveal it?

A: Because under the attorney-client privilege with Joan Storm I was not privileged to disclose this information until now.

He holds up a piece of paper.

Q: Please explain.

A: Miss Storm authorized me to disclose our conversation with regard to the general release. She did that out of sympathy for her father. She was confused as to whether she wanted him to be convicted. In a way she still loved him.

Q: Yes?

A: But she didn't authorize me to testify as to what happened two days later. Until now.

Q: What was that?

A: Two days later she returned to my office alone. She asked me to draft another document. This is it.

Q: Please read it to the jury.

A: "I, Joan Storm, hereby declare that the general release signed October 8, 1987, is void and of no consequence. It was signed under pressure and coercion.

"I declare under penalty of perjury this memorandum is true and correct. October 10, 1987. Signed, Joan Storm."

D.A.: You may examine.

Freitag: What made her change her mind about waiving the privilege?

A: It was when she heard you making your closing argument. You were scoring points with the jury with that general release. She realized this trial would be a sham unless the truth came out.

Q: Anything else?

A: Well . . . yes.

Q: What was it?

A: She just learned her father cut her out of his will.

————

Possible verdicts:

Paul Storm
1. Guilty of kidnapping
2. Not guilty

George McClure
1. Guilty of kidnapping
2. Not guilty

WHAT ARE YOUR VERDICTS?

[Before choosing your verdicts, see Jury Instructions 1–3, 5, 17, 19, 20, starting on page 197.]

QUESTIONS AND ANALYSIS

Q1.   Does a juror have the power to refuse to follow the law and vote not guilty, even if the facts support a guilty verdict?

Q2.   What is the real reason the judge did not allow the defense to show the alleged detriments of the Church of The Master—that is, why Dr. Storm believed the church was ruining his daughter's life?

Q3.   Should a person be allowed to commit a crime such as kidnapping when the motive is to save someone's life or well-being?

Q4.   By signing the general release, did Joan Storm actually release her father and George McClure from all criminal liability?

Q5.   Did the D.A. make a tactical error in prosecuting Dr. Storm and George McClure together?

———

A1.   The evidence against Dr. Storm and George McClure supported a guilty verdict under the law. They had no legal defense of justification or necessity. However, if a juror believes—as did some jurors in this case—that the law of kidnapping should not apply to Dr. Storm under these circumstances, or feels such sympathy for him that he or she cannot convict, then that juror has the power to vote for acquittal. This act of voting contrary to the law is called *jury nullification.*

Jurors take an oath to follow the law. Existing law, set forth by the Supreme Court in the 1895 case of *Sparf* v. *United States*, says juries must follow the law as explained by the judge. But while jurors do not have the *right* to disregard the law, they have the *power* to do so. Of course, jurors are not told of this power because courts do not wish to encourage it.

However, there are those in the legal community, including lawyers and judges, who believe judges should inform juries of their inherent right to decide not only the facts of a case but whether the law itself is unjust or misapplied. This group is still in the minority.

If a jury does nullify the law and votes not guilty where the facts support a guilty verdict under the law, the verdict cannot be appealed by the state no matter how strong the evidence. This is why prosecutors must take care to select jurors who will follow the law.

A2.   The real reason the judge did not allow defense counsel to show the alleged detriments of the Church of The Master, or all the reasons why Dr. Storm believed he had to save his daughter, is that such evidence would have turned the entire proceeding into a trial against the Church. Expert witnesses then would have been called to testify on both sides as to the good or bad of the organization. The jury's attention would have been diverted from the real issue—whether or not a kidnapping occurred. The consumption of time and the danger of confusing the jury were factors that persuaded the judge to keep out such evidence.

A3.   In rare cases the court might excuse the commission of a crime such as kidnapping if it is necessary to save someone's life or prevent great bodily harm. This is called *defense of necessity*. For example, the threat of attack by other inmates on a prisoner was recognized by the California court as a possible excuse for escape. However, in order for a defendant to use the defense of necessity, the physical danger must be imminent. In this case, the judge ruled the alleged threat to Joan Storm's life by the church as too remote to allow the defense.

A4.   Even if Joan Storm really intended to release her father and McClure from all criminal liability, she lacked the power to do so. The victim of a crime is not the one who decides if someone should be prosecuted. That decision lies with the D.A., who prosecutes on behalf of the people or the state. Of course, the D.A. may consider the victim's wishes, but the D.A. has the last word regardless of the victim's position.

A5.   See discussion under Verdict.

VERDICT

HUNG JURY AS TO BOTH DEFENDANTS

By prosecuting Dr. Storm and George McClure together, the D.A. probably made a tactical error. The difficulty of persuading a jury to convict a father of kidnapping his own daughter was simply too great for the prosecution to overcome. McClure benefited from being associated in the same case. The sympathy the jurors felt for Dr. Storm extended to McClure because they were tried together. Had McClure been tried separately, the state would have had a better chance of conviction.

The case was never tried again. The D.A. had the option to go forward with a retrial, but he chose not to do so.

STATE *v.* SCHAEFFER

You are juror number five, and Samuel Ringgold introduces himself as the deputy district attorney. He looks like the chairman of the board of a major corporation, and he speaks slowly and deliberately. In sharp contrast is defense attorney Tony Cipriano, so light on his feet he looks as if he's constantly holding himself back, nervous and ready for the starting gun.

"There is no dispute in this case," Ringgold says in his opening statement, "that this man, Kurt Schaeffer, shot and killed Larry Hansen on the morning of June 25, 1969, in the village of Del Centro. There is also no dispute that Larry Hansen was his best friend and business partner at the time. The only reason we are here pertains to the degree of the homicide—was it murder or manslaughter? We will prove it was murder, clear and simple, caused by not one, not two, but three bullets fired into Hansen's body."

You notice Schaeffer wince as Ringgold squeezes out the words "one . . . two . . . three."

The prosecution's first witness is police officer Robert Deming. He testifies that on the morning of June 25, while on duty in his patrol car, he was told by central dispatch that a man identifying himself as Kurt Schaeffer reported he had just shot his business partner and wanted the police to come and arrest him. The officer further states that he and Detective Gordon went to the office of the S&H Construction Company and found Kurt

Schaeffer waiting for them. Schaeffer indicated where his revolver was, on a shelf near the front door. The hammer of the gun was in a cocked position. Deming says Schaeffer was cooperative and full of remorse for what he had done.

Dr. Craig Fowler, county pathologist, is the next witness. He testifies that he examined the body and found three entry bullet wounds, one in the front of the left arm, one in the side of the neck, and one in the back.

The next witness is a short man in his middle sixties, Ben Simon. He is a cabinet maker who was working in his shop next to the defendant's construction office on the morning of the shooting when he heard what sounded like firecrackers. He gives the following answers to questions by the D.A.

Q: How many of these firecracker sounds did you hear?

A: Three. Bang! . . . Bang! Bang! Like that.

You notice a slight pause between the first and the second "bang."

Q: How much time went by between the three shots?

A: I really couldn't tell you.

Q: Well, just in your own words, using the words "bang, bang, bang." Again, tell us how you heard them with reference to the spacing between the shots. Just say it to yourself, slow, like this: "bang, bang"—

Cipriano jumps to his feet. "Your Honor, counsel is coaching the witness. I'd like to remind him the witness gives evidence, not him."

The judge replies, "Let him give his testimony, he has a right to. For the record, I'll time him." Turning to the witness, he says, "Will you repeat your testimony, with particular regard to the timing of the shots, and how much time passed between shots."

A: I said "bang" . . . I don't know, I'm confused, I don't know how fast I said it. I heard it . . . I don't know, I'm all mixed up.

D.A.: That's all. For the record, I'd like the statement of the witness to be recorded as the court heard it, with a full second between—

Cipriano again jumps to his feet, furious. To the D.A. he says, "You have no right to say what the evidence is, it's for the jury to decide how much time between shots."

The D.A. replies, equally furious, "I was merely trying to—"

The judge pounds his gavel, and you realize that the bang-bang testimony must be important. The judge states, "What the witness said has been heard by the jury, and the jury will disregard the remarks of counsel. Now we will take a ten-minute recess, during which I hope tempers will cool."

After the break, the judge returns and the trial resumes.

D.A.: I call Mrs. Vicki Schaeffer.

She is a small, thin, sandy-haired woman, and as she sits down in the witness stand she looks daggers at her husband, the defendant.

Q: You are Mrs. Kurt Schaeffer, the wife of the defendant? How long have you been married?

A: About eleven years.

In response to various questions, she testifies she had four children with Kurt Schaeffer, all girls, the youngest now only a year old and the oldest eight. She says the marriage went smoothly at first. Kurt was a good father and had a good job working in construction. About three years ago he started his own construction business with Larry Hansen, his best friend. In order to save money, Vicki worked in the office as secretary.

Q: Then the three of you were often in the office together?

A: Yes.

Q: What was your relationship with Larry?

A: At first he was just my husband's friend, but later on . . .

At this point she hesitates, searching for the right words.

A: I mean . . . well . . . it became something different.

Q: During this period, when Larry and your husband were running this construction company, did your married life change at all? That is, did you have any problems?

A: Oh, you mean Kurt's gambling? That started earlier. Kurt began to gamble, heavily. Horses and the dog races. And I told him he ought to stop, so he'd stop for a few days, and then it would get worse than ever.

She becomes emotional as she tells how Kurt bet larger and larger sums, that she tried to stop him, that they argued about it and their whole life changed; Kurt would lose his temper and yell at her. He became a different man, touchy and irritable, and although he promised to stop gambling, he never did. Finally she had to ask him for a divorce.

Q: Did he agree?

A: Not at first, but he finally gave in and moved out of the house.

Q: Then what?

A: He promised he'd join Gamblers Anonymous if I'd take him back. But I couldn't. Matters had gone too far and I . . . I was . . . in love with Larry.

Q: Was your husband aware of it?

A: I don't know. I couldn't tell him. I couldn't hurt him that much.

Q: Now I'd like to go back to the night before Larry was killed. Do you recall that night?

A: I hardly remember anything. It's all blacked out, it was such a terrible, horrible nightmare.

As she testifies, she becomes more and more upset and finally starts sobbing uncontrollably, whereupon the court orders a short recess.

After you return to the courtroom, Mrs. Schaeffer takes the stand again. She is quieter now, more in possession of herself, and the dialogue with the prosecutor continues.

Q: Do you understand, Mrs. Schaeffer, that since you are legally married to Kurt Schaeffer, you do not have to testify against him if you don't want to?

A: Yes, I understand. I want to testify.

Q: You had a conversation with your husband in your home early on the morning of June 25, 1969. What was it about?

A: He accused me of being out all night with Larry, and I told him it was none of his business where I was, that I had a right to do what I wanted.

Q: What is the next thing you recall?

A: He said he was going to kill me.

Q: And what did you say?

A: I don't know. It was awful, I couldn't believe it. I was hysterical, but I finally talked him out of it.

Q: Then what?

A: Then he called Larry all kinds of names and said he was going to kill him.

The prosecutor steps back and turns to Cipriano. "Your witness."

Cipriano hesitates, seems to study Mrs. Schaeffer, and then says quietly, "You hate the defendant, don't you, Mrs. Schaeffer?"

She reacts with an almost hysterical outburst. "Yes, I hate him. Hate— hate—hate! He killed the only man I ever loved!"

The defense counsel waits for her to quiet down. "You say you lived with your husband for eleven years and bore him four children, and yet you never loved him?"

The prosecutor jumps to his feet. "Objection, Your Honor. Irrelevant!" Before the judge can rule, Cipriano says quietly, "I will withdraw the question."

Q: Now, Mrs. Schaeffer, isn't it true that you told police investigators the morning after the murder that you couldn't remember anything that was said on the morning of June 25 between you and your husband?

A: Yes. I mean, I guess so. I forgot about that at first. I was so upset over Larry's death. They tell me I tried to kill myself. That's why they put me in the hospital.

Q: How long were you there, Mrs. Schaeffer?

A: They said I tried to throw myself down the canyon.

Her mind seems to be wandering, and the question is repeated.

Q: How long were you in the hospital?

A: I think it was five weeks.

Q: And how much time passed before you remembered this threat made by your husband to kill Larry?

A: I don't know.

Q: Was it after you were out of the hospital?

A: Yes.

Q: Actually you were out of the hospital a week when you first mentioned this threat. You hadn't remembered it until then, right?

A: You know what I'm going to say. Yes, yes, yes!

Q: Just one or two more questions. Did you tell your husband when he was leaving that night that Hansen was a better lover than he ever was?

A: I don't know. I don't recall.

Q: Try to recall. "Larry's a better lover than you ever were." Is it possible you said it?

"Objection, Your Honor. Anything is possible."

"Sustained."

Q: All right. Is it probable you said it?

A: I may have said it, I could have said it, I don't recall.

Cipriano stands still for a moment, letting the answer sink in.

"Thank you, Mrs. Schaeffer. That is all."

The judge calls a recess for lunch. When court resumes, the prosecution calls Mrs. Schaeffer's older sister, Adelheid Hoffman. She is a Brunhilde type, tall and strong-boned. She testifies she was babysitting for Vicki that evening and was sleeping on the couch downstairs. The children's room was upstairs, as was Vicki's. Earlier in the evening Vicki went out to meet Larry Hansen, and about 2:00 A.M. Mrs. Hoffman woke up to find Kurt Schaeffer standing beside her. He wanted to know where Vicki was. He was upset and said he'd make her feel sorry, she had no right to do this to him.

Q: Did he say how he was going to make her feel sorry?

A: He said he was going to kill her and Larry and then kill himself.

Q: What did you do then?

A: I was shocked. We talked. Talked for a long time. After a while he calmed down and said he'd forget everything if only he could get her back. Then the phone rang.

Q: Who was it?

A: It was Vicki, and she said she was coming home. I started to tell her that Kurt was here, but he grabbed the phone. He asked her where she was, but she hung up on him. Then without saying anything he turned around and left the house.

Q: Then what?

A: A few minutes later Vicki came home and went upstairs to her bedroom, without even speaking to me. I lay down and tried to get some sleep, but Kurt came back. He walked right past me as if he didn't even see me and rushed upstairs, and I could hear them talking.

Q: What did they say?

A: I couldn't hear their words, but they were yelling at each other, and after a while Kurt came down. He came down the stairs slowly, and Vicki came to the top of the stairs and shouted something. After he left, I heard Vicki talking to Larry on the phone and telling him that Kurt was on his way to the office.

Q: Thank you, that's all.

Cipriano stands up to say he has only a few questions.

Q: You and Kurt were good friends. You knew that he loved Vicki very much, and you tried to bring about a reconciliation. Is that right?

A: Yes.

Q: You didn't like Larry?

"Objection! Irrelevant."

"Sustained!"

Q: You could tell Kurt was very upset that night?

A: Oh yes. Especially when he left the last time. He was shaking.

Q: Out of control?

"Objection! Calls for a conclusion."

The judge pauses. He looks undecided. Finally he says, "Overruled. You may answer."

A: Yes. You could say that.

Q: In a heat of passion?

A: Yes.

"That's all, thank you."

Mr. Ringgold rises as if he wants to ask more questions, but then he just waves his hand and sits back. "The State rests."

Cipriano opens his case for the defense. Various witnesses, including several prominent citizens of the town of Del Centro, testify that Kurt Schaeffer had a good reputation in the community as a peaceful, law-abiding and honest person; that he loved his wife and children very much and desperately wanted his wife back.

Now Kurt Schaeffer takes the stand amid a murmur of expectation. He is a good-looking, burly man, about thirty-three years old. He has a short beard and blue, glassy eyes. He tries not to look at his wife sitting in the back row.

After a few preliminary questions in which Schaeffer identifies himself and states how he and Larry Hansen started a business together and were building it up, his attorney comes to the question of the gun.

Q: Did you have a permit for it?

A: No.

Q: Then you bought it illegally?

A: No. I found it in a junk pile, about two years ago. It was an old gun and I took it. It was rusty and I didn't know whether it would work, but I cleaned it and oiled it and saw that it would operate.

Q: And what did you do with the gun?

A: I kept it under my mattress, to protect my family.

Q: Now, Mr. Schaeffer, I'd like to get to the day this tragedy occurred. Where were you that night?

A: I went to a meeting of Gamblers Anonymous. I felt I was making progress, and I wanted to tell my wife, so I went to her house, only she wasn't there, but her sister Addie was, and the kids were sleeping upstairs. Addie and I talked.

Q: You heard her say you talked of killing your wife and Larry, then yourself, didn't you? Is that true?

A: If she said it, I guess it's true. I don't know—

Q: But then isn't it also true that you calmed down and put aside those thoughts of killing—

Ringgold jumps to his feet.

"Objection, Your Honor! He is leading the witness. I have no objection to the defendant telling his story. But let it come from him, not his attorney."

"Sustained. Proceed, Mr. Cipriano."

Q: All right, just tell us what happened next.

A: The phone rang. Addie answered, but I knew it was Vicki and I grabbed it. I tried to talk to her but she hung up on me. So I left.

Q: Where did you go then?

A: I figured they were at Larry's place, so I drove out that way. Then I saw our truck, the red one, coming the other way. Larry was driving. There was somebody with him. I thought it was Vicki, so I turned around and went back to the house. The truck was gone but I knew Vicki was inside, so I went back in.

Q: You talked to Vicki then?

A: Yes. I told her I had to have her back. I said things . . . I don't remember. I was upset . . . but she . . . she looked at me as if she'd never seen me before . . . she said she was in love with Larry and they wanted the divorce. I can't remember . . .

He stops talking. You can see the tears in his eyes. The judge waits, and presently Schaeffer looks up and wipes his eyes. He is staring straight ahead.

Cipriano: Can you go on?

A: Go ahead.

Q: Do you remember her saying Larry was a better lover than you?

A: No . . . I mean . . . yes. I . . . she couldn't. I—

Q: You don't want to remember that, do you?

"Objection! Leading."

"Sustained."

Q: Did she say it?

There is a long pause.

A: Yes.

This time the judge orders a recess. When the questioning resumes, Schaeffer seems like a different man. He is cold, without emotion, and he answers in a matter-of-fact voice.

Q: What happened after you left the house?

A: I went to the office. I was hoping Larry wouldn't be there. I just wanted to kill myself. But when I walked in and saw Larry there grinning at me and saying he wanted to talk to me, and then I don't know, I shot him. I tried to shoot myself, only the gun jammed. That's all I can remember.

Cipriano turns around and speaks to the prosecutor.

"You may inquire, Counselor."

On cross-examination, Schaeffer is often confused. Ringgold presses him to recall what his intentions were while he was driving around that night, while he was at the house, after he left Vicki, but he can't remember. He can't remember at what point he got the gun. He wasn't in control of himself. He apologizes to the court for not being able to remember.

"I am sorry, sir," he says to Mr. Ringgold. "But it's all a jumble in my mind. I want to tell the truth. I . . ." There is a long pause. "I did it. It was wrong. I deserve to be punished."

The last witness for the defense is Dr. Basil Bernard, a clinical psychologist, who gives his opinion that Schaeffer was incapable of exercising adequate control over his responses to environmental stimuli. He testifies that tests showed Kurt's personality was noteworthy for the repeated themes of masculine inadequacy, and this feeling motivated him to keep a gun under his mattress in order to give him a sense of masculine power. Kurt also hoped to improve his worth through gambling, but he was not successful.

The doctor then concludes his testimony by stating that Schaeffer's mental capacity was diminished at the time of the shooting to the point where he could not maturely and deliberately premeditate and reflect on the gravity of his act. He was in such a mental state, such heat of passion, that he could not really think about what he was doing or what it meant.

The cross-examination adds little, after which the defense rests.

In rebuttal the prosecution calls a psychiatrist, Dr. Conrad Friedrich, to the stand. Unlike the younger Dr. Bernard, Dr. Friedrich is a licensed physician. He says he saw Schaeffer the day of the shooting, and he concludes that Schaeffer was legally sane at the time of the shooting in that "he could distinguish the difference between right and wrong and was aware of the nature and quality of his act." The doctor says he thought Schaeffer could meaningfully premeditate on the gravity of his act.

Cipriano starts cross-examination with a gentle voice.

Q: Let me get this straight, Doctor. You say he *could* premeditate on what he was doing?

A: He could, yes, he had the mental capacity to premeditate.

Q: But you are only saying he had the ability to do so.

A: Yes.

Q: You cannot say he did?

A: No. No evidence of that. I think it was an impulsive, spur-of-the-moment act.

Q: In the heat of passion?

A: One might say that.

Q: Thank you, Doctor.

The D.A. has further questions: "This 'heat of passion' counsel asked you about: you have no way of knowing how strong—how hot—that was, do you, Doctor?"

"Well . . ." The doctor looks through his records. "The police gave me a letter they found in his pocket. Oh, yes, here it is." Dr. Friedrich draws out a crumpled sheet of paper. "Shall I read it, Your Honor?"

Both attorneys rush to the witness stand to look at the letter in the doctor's hands. It is apparent neither has seen it before. They study it over the doctor's shoulder, then walk back to their seats.

Defense counsel: No objection.

D.A.: [weakly] No objection.

The doctor reads aloud: "My heart is aching so bad since my separation from my wife and children, I cannot bear it. I keep praying night after night she will come back to me. Perhaps if my love for her was not so strong and deep I could go along. But I cannot. If I have to live apart from my family, I shall ask God, Our Father, to end my life, merciful soon. Signed, Kurt Schaeffer."

Defense counsel: The date, Doctor, of that letter?

A: June 18, 1969.

Q: One week before the shooting?

A: Yes.

"That's all."

———

Possible verdicts:

1. Guilty of first degree murder
2. Guilty of second degree murder
3. Guilty of voluntary manslaughter
4. Not guilty

WHAT IS YOUR VERDICT?

[Before choosing your verdict, see Jury Instructions 1–3, 5–14, starting on page 197.]

QUESTIONS AND ANALYSIS

Q1. What finding by the county pathologist was extremely damaging to the defense?

Q2. Why was the length of time between the three "bangs" so important?

Q3. Why did the defense attorney insist on bringing out the taunting remark by Schaeffer's wife that Hansen was a better lover?

Q4. How did the letter found in Schaeffer's pocket help the defense?

———

A1. The most damaging piece of evidence against the defendant was the pathologist's finding that Hansen was shot in the back. Schaeffer testified he remembered Hansen grinning at him just before the shots were fired. If so, that meant Hansen must have turned around to flee after Schaeffer opened fire and then was shot in the back, a powerful piece of circumstantial evidence tending to show a deliberate and premeditated intent to kill.

A2. The length of time between the three shots was an important issue because it could show whether the defendant thought about what he was doing between each shot, or fired so rapidly he didn't have time to think. Ben Simon's testimony indicated that there was a pause between the first and second shots. Time to think before the fatal shot is a circumstance supporting the element of deliberation and premeditation necessary for first degree murder.

A3. The realistic goal of the defense attorney in this case was to reduce the killing from murder to manslaughter. He knew he had no chance for acquittal. In order to do this, the defense had to show that Schaeffer was provoked by some incident that would naturally arouse the heat of passion of an ordinary, reasonable man in the same circumstances. Vicki Schaeffer's remark—"Larry's a better lover than you ever were"—is arguably the kind of provocation that would make a husband act rashly and thus reduce the crime to manslaughter.

A4.   The letter found in Schaeffer's pocket was helpful to his defense because it showed the extent of his depression over the loss of his wife. One of the laws existing at the time of this trial was "Diminished Capacity." Under this law jurors were told that if the defendant's mental capacity was diminished to the point where they had a reasonable doubt whether he could maturely and meaningfully reflect upon the gravity of his act, then they could not find him guilty of first degree murder. Schaeffer's suicidal depression shown by the letter might be considered some evidence of such diminished mental capacity.

VERDICT

GUILTY OF MURDER
IN THE SECOND DEGREE

There was no question in the minds of the jurors that Schaeffer intended to kill and did kill Hansen. The dispute that went on for several days in the jury room was whether the verdict should be Murder in the First Degree or a lesser degree of homicide such as Murder in the Second Degree or Voluntary Manslaughter.

The difference in terms of penalty can be substantial. The maximum sentence for first degree murder in a non-capital case is generally life in prison while the most one can get for manslaughter is usually about ten years. The numbers vary in different states.

Certain jurors could not vote for first degree murder because of doubts as to Schaeffer's mental state at the time of the shooting. Some could not put aside their sympathy for his position in the love triangle. As a result the jury compromised on second degree murder.

The argument for voluntary manslaughter based on heat of passion failed to carry the jury, because jurors felt sufficient time elapsed between the moment Schaeffer left the house and his arrival at the crime scene for such passions to cool.

(Sentence: Five Years to Life in Prison)

STATE v. ANDREWS

Jury Selection in a Capital Case

You are potential juror number six in a capital case, which means the state is seeking the death penalty. You are not a juror yet, because jury selection is still in progress.

Damon Andrews is charged with the murder of a nineteen-year-old girl. He is also charged with the special circumstance of committing rape on the victim during the commission of the murder.

The Deputy District Attorney is Alice Gentry, a petite, cheerful-looking woman with shoulder-length hair, which she continually brushes off her face.

"I will tell you right now," she says in a soft, gentle voice, "I am going to ask you to return the death penalty in this case. Can you do that?"

You are still in a state of shock. Since this was your first time on jury duty, you thought you would get something like a traffic violation. You were caught off guard when you heard the charges.

You look at the defendant, a rotund little blond man, trying not to stare. He sits between his defense team of two attorneys; on the one side, chestnut-haired Natalie Blake; on the other, tall Craig Mirtaw. During this jury selection, the two are constantly exchanging hastily written notes, sliding them across the table in front of the man whose life is in their hands.

But it is the judge who is asking the questions.

"If the case reaches the penalty phase," the judge says, "you will have to choose, and choose fairly, between two possible sentences: life in prison without possibility of parole, or death in the gas chamber."

The judge looks at each of you in the jury box. "Can you do that?"

You've thought about the death penalty before. You've discussed it with your family at home. But you never thought you personally would have to decide if someone should live or die. When the issue was put to the voters in the last election, you voted to support capital punishment. But this feels different. If you are chosen, the choice will be in your hands. You will decide, if the case goes that far, if the man sitting a few feet away should be put to death in the gas chamber or spend the rest of his life in prison.

You look at him again. You ask yourself, "Can I do that?"

"This case will begin as any other criminal case," the judge says. "You will hear the evidence and the law. Then you will decide if the defendant is guilty of murder beyond a reasonable doubt or not guilty of murder."

The judge steps down from the bench and moves to a big chart on the wall, which he uses as he explains the step-by-step process that leads up to the final life or death decision. (See opposite page.)

You and about fifty other prospective jurors are jammed into the courtroom. Your name was called with eleven others from the panel to sit in the jury box for final questioning by the judge. The others are waiting to take your place if one of you stumbles in your answer and is excused. Along with other members of the panel you struggled to fill out a twenty-eight-page questionnaire that took you over an hour to complete. Now the judge has narrowed the questioning to one single question, your ability to fairly consider the penalty of death.

"If, and only if," the judge says, "you decide he is guilty of murder, you go to the second decision—whether he is guilty of first degree murder or second degree murder. If, and only if, you find he is guilty of first degree murder, you go to the third decision and decide if the special circumstance of rape or attempted rape is true. If you find it is not true, you will stop—notice the stop sign—and there will be no consideration of penalty. But if, and, I repeat, only if, you find the special circumstance is true, then we

JURORS' DECISIONS FROM
GUILT PHASE TO PENALTY PHASE

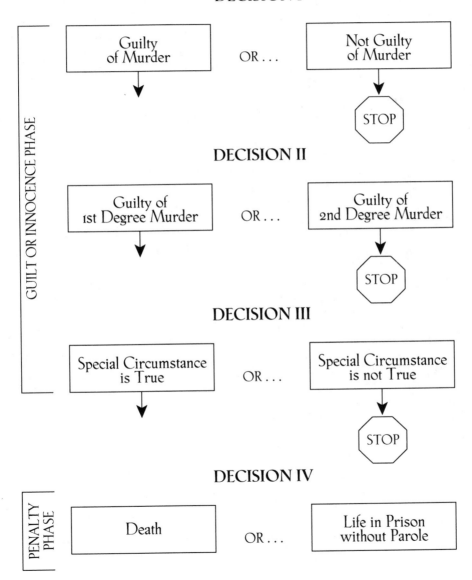

will have a separate phase, a second trial, immediately following the guilt phase. This second trial is the penalty phase and will never be reached unless you pass through all the steps I have described.

"In the penalty phase, if we get there, you will hear additional evidence; aggravating factors showing why he should die, mitigating factors showing why he should live. Then you will go out to the jury room again and decide whether the aggravating factors are so substantial in comparison to the mitigating factors that death is warranted. If so, you would return the verdict of death; if not, you would return the verdict of life in prison without possibility of parole."

Some prospective jurors opposed to the death penalty in any case have already been excused. They told the judge they could not vote for it no matter how strong the evidence. Several others said they would automatically vote for death if the defendant was proved guilty of committing first degree murder and raping the victim during the murder. They were also excused. But there are still some who are on the fence.

The judge turns and faces prospective juror number one, a middle-aged woman, at the other end of your row. She tells the judge she has always been a homemaker, raised three children, and never worked outside the home.

"Mrs. Lawrence," the judge says to her, "some people have told us they believe in the death penalty, but they personally could not give the verdict of death to anyone. They just couldn't do it. We need to know where you stand."

"I guess I've lived a sheltered life," she says, "but I believe in the death penalty. I think I'm fair."

"Do you understand that if your verdict is death, then, as a juror, you must accept the fact that is what will happen. He will be put to death. If your verdict is life in prison without possibility of parole, you must also accept that is what will happen. He will be in prison for the rest of his life. You must be able to accept that no matter what you have read or heard about such cases. Can you do that?"

Juror #1: That's a hard question, Judge. I'm not sure I could.

Judge: What do you mean by that?

Juror #1: When you put it that way . . . I mean, when I think of someone's life at stake, I really don't know how I would feel when it comes right down to it, right down to where I'd have to decide—life or death. I want to do my civic duty. But it would affect me. It would weigh heavy on my mind. Be a lot of stress on me.

Judge: I'm not saying it would be easy, Mrs. Lawrence. It would be troubling to anyone. That doesn't make you a bad juror. Anyone who has to choose between another human being's life or death, that's a difficult decision. It may trouble you a great deal.

Juror #1: I'm sure it would.

Judge: But what we have to know is: could you be fair to both sides in making that decision—fair to the people of this state who have made the death penalty their law, and fair also to this defendant?

Juror #1: Judge, I'd be fair in every way I could.

Judge: And if you come to that penalty stage and the facts are so strong that in your mind they warrant the death penalty, could you return to this courtroom and look this man in the eye and say: "Mr. Andrews, you must die for what you did"? Could you do that, knowing that is what would happen—he would then be put to death in the gas chamber? Could you do that?

Juror #1 pauses. She stares at the judge.

Juror #1: I'd have to wait and see, Judge. I never thought about it that way before.

Judge: I am asking you to think about it now.

Juror #1: I'm trying to be honest . . .

Judge: The problem is, Mrs. Lawrence, we cannot wait and see. We have to know now. The D.A., the defense attorney, the defendant, yes, the people of this state, they have a right to know now.

Juror #1: Judge, please understand me, I can't say now. Not until I heard the evidence.

Judge: Now wait a minute. I'm not asking you to decide now what you're going to do. I am not asking that question. Please listen to my question. My question is this: If, and I repeat, if the evidence is strong enough to warrant the death penalty—notice I said *if*—and knowing that if you return such a verdict he would die in the gas chamber, if that is the situation, could you return that verdict of death? Could you do that?

Juror #1: Judge, let me answer it this way. To the best of my belief I think I could. But to state one way or another now, I can't honestly say. I'd have to wait and see before I decide—

Judge: But I'm not asking you to decide—

Juror #1: I understand—

Judge: Look, the attorneys, this defendant, they have a right to know now. Before this trial begins. They have a right to know now if you can follow the law. Because if we went to trial and you heard the evidence, and the evidence strongly warranted the death penalty, and then you said, "No, no matter what the evidence is, I could not do that," that would be unfair to the people of this state.

Juror #1: Judge, I believe I could be fair to the people of this state. I believe I could be fair to this man here. And if he is guilty, if the facts were strong enough, it would hurt me terribly, but I could do it. I wouldn't want to do it. There would be extreme pressure.

Judge: What extreme pressure?

Juror #1: Judge, a man's life is at stake.

Judge: Yes.

Juror #1: I would do what I had to do, regardless of how much it hurt me. But it would bother me bad. I'm the type of person it would bother real bad. But I could do it. I'm sorry I'm disappointing you with my answers.

Judge: It's not a matter of disappointing me. I just need to know how you feel down deep.

Juror #1: I know, Judge, but I don't see how any person could sit in this seat and give an answer one way or another.

Judge: I'm not asking you to decide now—

Juror #1: I just couldn't give an answer.

Judge: Thank you, Mrs. Lawrence. I will excuse you from this case. Thank you for being open with us. We'll call another juror.

The clerk picks a name at random from her box and calls out the name of Bernard Maltz. A heavyset man in his sixties, Mr. Maltz takes the seat left vacant by Mrs. Lawrence. The questioning goes more smoothly this time.

". . . and if you were a juror in the penalty phase," the judge says, "could you accept the rule that you must not consider, not even for an instant, the relative cost or expense to the taxpayer of either one of the penalties—life in prison or death? Do you understand it would be improper for you to consider the relative expense in reaching your verdict?"

New Juror #1: I understand.

Judge: And the law also states that your decision must be based upon what is the proper punishment for this particular defendant. That means you may not consider any deterrent value to others; can you do that?

New Juror #1: Judge, I always thought the purpose of the death penalty was deterrence.

Judge: No, not in this state. Whatever you may have thought, you must set such thoughts aside and reach your penalty verdict based solely on the question: what is the proper penalty for this defendant? Whether it deters anyone must not be part of your thinking. Can you do that?

New Juror #1: I understand now, yes. I can do that.

Judge: Nor what sort of message your verdict will send out to the community. You can't consider that, either. That too must not be part of your thinking. Can you do that? Can you follow that law?

New Juror #1: I will, yes.

Judge: And I want you to understand that there is no such thing as an automatic death sentence or automatic sentence of life in prison without parole. You can reach the decision on penalty only through this process that I have described, as illustrated on this chart, through this gradual step-by-step process. You understand that?

New Juror #1: Yes, I do.

Judge: And one last question, Mr. Maltz. I want you to search your heart, your mind, your soul, and I want you to tell us: do you have any personal beliefs, whether they be based on religion or morals or politics or philosophy, that would prevent you from being fair?

New Juror #1: I've thought about it. No, Your Honor, there is nothing to keep me from being fair.

The judge turns to prospective juror number two, but before he can speak the man is on his feet.

Juror #2: May I say something, Your Honor?

Judge: Yes.

Juror #2: Your Honor, there is something you should know before you begin.

Judge: Yes?

Juror #2: I believe in the death penalty. In fact I strongly support it. But I don't believe in the gas chamber. I don't think that's the humane way to kill a man.

Judge: Are you saying that if this case reaches the penalty phase, you could not vote for the death penalty, no matter how strong the evidence was?

Juror #2: That's right, Your Honor. So long as it's death in the gas chamber.

Judge: You realize this state has specifically chosen the gas chamber as its method of execution?

Juror #2: I didn't choose it. I just don't believe in killing a man with gas. I believe it should be by injection of some type.

Judge: Well, thank you for telling us.

Juror #2: Does it have to be by the gas chamber, Your Honor?

Judge: That's the law in this state. You will be excused. I will ask the clerk to call another name.

The new juror number two, plus jurors number three and number four, go through the questioning without problems. You feel the pressure as it gets closer to your turn. Juror number five, seated on your left, tells the judge he is a retired professor of economics.

Judge: Do you understand that if you reach the penalty phase and you have to choose between death and life in prison, you are not allowed to consider, not even for an instant, the relative cost or expense to the taxpayer of either penalty?

Juror #5: That's hard to separate out, Judge. It's costing the American people billions to support all these prisoners on life sentences.

Judge: Under the law you must separate it out, you must not let it enter into your deliberations.

Juror #5: I could try, but . . . it's costing us a lot of money. If we can execute these folks, that sounds a lot cheaper to me.

Judge: You haven't made any study of which penalty costs the most, have you?

Juror #5: No, I just took it for granted that life in prison is more expensive. And if I sat on this case and I had to choose between the two, I might think some poor child is being denied medical care because of the expense of giving a murderer life in prison without parole instead of death. In that case I think I would take the expense into account.

Judge: Thank you, sir. You will be excused.

Juror number five is replaced by a middle-aged woman, a sixth-grade teacher who says she is a member of the ACLU but doesn't agree with the ACLU's stand on the death penalty.

Judge: Are you saying you're in favor of the death penalty?

New Juror #5: I just think it's proper in certain cases. It doesn't mean I favor it. In fact I don't like it. I voted against it in the election.

Judge: But you could impose it—

New Juror #5: Yes—

Judge: If the evidence is so strong that it calls for it . . . warrants it?

New Juror #5: Ten years ago I would have said no, I could never do it. But times have changed. Sometimes we have to do what we don't want to do . . . Yes . . . Now I could do it.

Judge: Even though you are generally opposed to it?

New Juror #5: That's right . . . I'd have to put those feelings aside.

The judge looks at her for a long moment.

Judge: Could you do that? Could you promise me you would give both sides a fair hearing?

New Juror #5: I promise . . . Yes . . . I could be fair.

The judge turns to you. "What we are looking for," he says, "are jurors who can consider the two possible penalties—life or death—with an open mind, without leaning one way or another until you have heard the evidence."

You are squirming in your seat.

"Can you do that?"

QUESTIONS AND ANALYSIS

Q1. The law requires that the jury in a capital case be made up solely of persons willing to impose the death penalty and excludes all persons who could not. Is this fair?

Q2. What about Mrs. Lawrence, the potential juror who was dismissed by the judge? She said she could be fair but that she'd have to wait and see if she could impose the death penalty, even if the facts were strong enough to warrant it. The judge said, "We cannot wait and see. We have to know now." Was it right for the judge to dismiss her?

Q3. The judge told potential jurors that in order to serve on the jury they must be able to accept that their decision as to life or death is what will happen, i.e., if they vote for death, then the defendant will be put to death in the gas chamber; if they vote for life in prison, then the defendant will be imprisoned for the rest of his life. The law required the judge to make this statement. Could you follow such an instruction if you were a juror?

Q4. If you are generally opposed to the idea of the death penalty, does that mean you would be automatically excluded from serving as a juror in a capital case?

Q5. Many prospective jurors in capital cases take it for granted that the sentence of life in prison without parole is much more costly to the taxpayer than the death penalty. Is this a valid assumption?

———

A1. Many legal scholars say this exclusion is unfair. They cite studies showing that a jury composed only of those willing to impose the death penalty and excluding all those who would not, is a jury more likely to find the defendant guilty. The argument is that the defendant is thereby denied a fair cross-section of the community, a jury of his or her peers. Whatever the validity of this view and the alleged unfairness of the law, the reality is simply this: if the law allowed persons unalterably opposed to capital punishment to sit on the jury, the state could never obtain a verdict of death.

A2.   The judge's decision to dismiss Mrs. Lawrence was a close call. The D.A. would agree with him because of Mrs. Lawrence's ambivalence on voting for death. The defense would object on the grounds she said she could be fair, and that no one can really be sure how he or she would feel until actually faced with the choice. Other judges could go either way. The scene illustrates the difficulty of obtaining acceptable jurors in a death penalty case.

A3.   Because of public knowledge that death penalty appeals often take many years, that verdicts can be reversed on appeal or commuted by the governor, jurors find it difficult to accept the judge's statement that their verdict of life or death will be carried out. The law requires jurors to take this position, however, out of concern that a wavering juror will cast a vote thinking someone higher up will make the final decision.

A4.   The fact that a prospective juror is generally opposed to the death penalty does not mean such a person will be automatically excluded from being a juror. There are those who have general objections to the death penalty but can still follow the law and return such a verdict if the facts are strong enough. The Supreme Court has ruled they can still be on the jury so long as the judge is satisfied they can set their feeling of opposition aside and give both sides a fair hearing.

A5.   Jurors are not allowed to consider the relative cost or expense to the taxpayer of the death penalty as compared to life in prison without parole. Any opinions on that issue must also be set aside. Many Americans assume the death penalty is much less expensive to the public than life in prison. Although research is still going on, most legal scholars say the assumption is false, that the death penalty costs much more because of all the procedural safeguards required by the Constitution to protect the defendant and ensure a fair process. Studies in New York and Florida set the cost of each capital case upward from $1.4 million to $3.2 million, which is at least twice what it would cost to keep a defendant in prison for life.

What we see in this brief section on jury selection in a capital case is only a small portion of the exhaustive questioning, oral and written, which goes on in every trial where death is a possible verdict. The law requires a heightened level of due process be afforded the capital defendant. Every step, from arrest to appeal to the execution itself, demands more time and attention from all sides.

Although there have been many attempts to speed up the process, some courts in death-penalty states will still take weeks, even months, to pick the jury. Attorneys feel they must explore every attitude that might affect a juror's final life-or-death choice. Certain judges will allow individual questioning, bringing each prospective juror into the courtroom alone outside the presence of the others in order to encourage more open responses rather than the usual procedure with the entire panel present. For certain delicate subjects, such as a potential juror's personal experiences with rape or child molestation, the judge will invite the prospective juror into the privacy of chambers for a closed hearing.

The United States Supreme Court has recognized that the death penalty is unique in severity and finality.

"Death," the Supreme Court says, "is different."

STATE v. SARKO

You are juror number seven on a case in which Stephen Sarko, who is homosexual, is charged with the murder of his roommate, Leo Melnik, also gay.

Since the defendant is an admitted homosexual, the question of any prejudice you might have for or against gays has been explored in jury selection.

"I will ask one more time," Judge Grayson says to the jury. "Is there any member of this jury who has any bias or prejudice toward homosexual persons that might prevent you from being fair in this case?"

You glance at the defendant again. You see nothing that would indicate his sexual orientation. He is trim, athletic-looking—yes, even masculine.

The judge waits. No one answers. "Good," he says. "Swear the jury."

D.A. Jack Kornbluth makes his opening statement. "He may not look like a murderer now," he says, "but I assure you he will look different to you when you hear what he did."

Sarko's attorney is Tom O'Connor, a man you remember from your service as a juror in the case of State v. Washburn *(page 37)*. He is the white-haired Irishman who was a D.A. until he threatened to fight the judge. Then he became a defense attorney.

"What Stephen Sarko did," O'Connor says, "was help his dying friend commit suicide. That is all. What we have here is not murder of any kind but an act of friendship and love."

The prosecution calls Linda Keely as its first witness. She is the director of nursing at Valley Hospital. Leo Melnik was a practical nurse on her staff. He failed to show up for work on the evening of October 11, 1991, which was unusual for him. When he didn't show up the following evening she became concerned. Her phone calls to his number were unanswered, so she called the police and asked them to check his apartment.

On cross-examination by O'Connor she states that her staff has to treat patients who have AIDS.

Q: You are aware that AIDS is almost always fatal?

A: Yes.

Q: Once you have it, you are likely to die?

A: In many cases, right.

Q: Did Leo Melnik have AIDS?

A: I have no idea.

Q: Was he ever tested for AIDS?

A: You mean by our hospital?

Q: Yes—before you hired him?

A: No. We cannot demand that an individual be tested for AIDS. That might be considered discrimination. So we don't do it.

Eva Melnik takes the stand. She is the victim's mother. Mrs. Melnik lives in Moberly, Missouri. She testifies her son left his hometown in Missouri while still in his teens, when he realized he was homosexual. He moved to the West Coast to be in a friendlier atmosphere, where he lived for the past seventeen years. She often discussed his homosexuality openly with him. She knows he attempted suicide three years ago, but he never told her he had AIDS. As far as she knew he was in good health, even ran several miles a day to stay in shape. She also phoned the police when she couldn't reach him on the phone.

Tom Jessup testifies he was the first police officer on the scene. He received a radio call in his patrol car on the evening of October 11, 1991, to check on a Leo Melnik in an apartment at 2005 Fifth Avenue. When he rang the bell and banged on the door without getting an answer, he inquired of neighbors. They said they hadn't seen Melnik or his roommate, Stephen Sarko, for several days.

Finally, Officer Jessup kicked in the door. Seeing no one in the living room, he opened the door to the bedroom. There, lying on the bed, face-down on the pillow, was a fully clothed man who fit the description of Leo Melnik. The officer checked for rigor mortis. He felt the skin, lifted an arm and let it drop, and determined Melnik had been dead several hours. Melnik's hands were behind his back, but they were not tied. The officer found no ropes or bindings of any kind. He saw no blood on the bed or anywhere else in the apartment. He searched the apartment for possible murder weapons but found none.

While he was still in the apartment the phone rang, and he answered it. It was Melnik's mother calling from Missouri, asking to speak with her son. The officer had to tell her the truth. "That," he says, "was one of the hardest things I ever had to do."

Another police officer, Detective Christine Cusimano, is called to the stand. She was a member of the homicide team investigating the case. Officer Cusimano arrived on the scene soon after receiving Officer Jessup's call for assistance. She inspected the body, noticed abrasions on the wrists and ligature marks across the front of the throat. In her opinion these marks were caused by a tightening of an object such as a rope around the neck. The apartment was neat, showing no sign of a struggle, no sign of any forced entry. She found a card on the desk that read: "AIDS and the DOCTORS OF DEATH. Dr. Marvin Rosenberg."

Investigation led Cusimano's team to Sarko in his cousin's apartment across town. When they found him, he seemed very frightened. After being advised of his rights, Sarko admitted he had been Melnik's room-mate, that he helped him commit suicide, then left the body on the bed because he was afraid of the consequences. He broke down in tears and refused to answer any more questions without the advice of an attorney. He was placed under arrest and charged with murder.

Dr. David Zuniga testifies as the medical examiner who performed the autopsy. The cause of death was asphyxia by ligature strangulation. He found ligature marks on the neck, bruising of the tongue by the teeth of a clenched mouth, and ligature marks on the wrists. Dr. Zuniga also examined the victim's colon. He found purple spots in the intestines, and after examining them under a microscope he concluded Melnik had been suffering from a cancer called Kaposi's sarcoma. The doctor testifies this is an indication the decedent was infected with the AIDS virus.

D.A. Kornbluth hones in on the AIDS question.

Q: You are certain Mr. Melnik tested positive for the HIV virus associated with AIDS?

A: Yes.

Q: Does that mean he was going to die from it?

A: Not necessarily. Some people with this virus may never get sick.

Q: They could live indefinitely?

A: Yes.

Q: Through their natural course in life?

A: It's possible, yes.

Q: And when people die of AIDS, do they die because their immune system breaks down?

A: Yes.

Q: And do they suffer from various illnesses before death?

A: Yes—usually pneumonia, sometimes malignancies, until they finally succumb to some fatal infection.

Q: And did you see any evidence that Mr. Melnik suffered from pneumonia or any other serious illness before his death?

A: I did not.

Q: And he was of normal weight for his size?

A: His weight was normal. There was no indication of any abnormal weight loss.

O'Connor begins cross-examination with a hypothetical question.

Q: Doctor, if a man's wrists were bound behind his back, and a cord was wrapped around his neck and tied to his wrists, would it be possible for that person to choke himself to death?

A: It's possible. But doubtful.

Q: Why do you say doubtful, Doctor?

A: Because usually a person will lapse into unconsciousness first before dying from strangulation. And so it's unlikely that while unconscious he would be able to keep up the pressure or tension necessary to strangle himself to death.

Q: But it could happen?

A: Possible.

The prosecution rests.

Now Stephen Sarko takes the stand in his defense, a frightened look on his face.

O'Connor starts right off with the fact that Sarko is gay.

Q: Let's start with your sexual orientation. What is that?

A: I am a homosexual.

Q: How long have you been a homosexual?

A: All of my life.

Q: When do you first recall having a homosexual encounter?

A: I had encounters at five or six.

He testifies he was working in a bookstore around the time of Melnik's death. A year before meeting Leo Melnik, he had been involved with a man named Eddie Wilmont. They were not only lovers but best friends. Then Eddie contracted AIDS. As his illness became serious, he asked Sarko to live with him, to help him in his final days. So Sarko moved in with Eddie, tended his needs, took him to the hospital. Sarko watched the horror of the ordeal, how Eddie suffered. After Eddie died he moved back to his own place and began looking for another friend and lover. One day when he was about to cross the street near the park a car went by slowly and the driver cruised him.

Q: What do you mean, he "cruised" you?

A: He looked me up and down. He did certain things with his eyes.

Q: What did you do in response?

A: I looked at him the same way.

Q: This form of cruising—is that a common experience?

A: Everybody does it.

Q: How many times have you been cruised like that?

A: Hundreds of times.

Sarko says the driver turned the car around and asked him where he was going, and he got in. They went to the apartment of the driver, Leo Melnik, and that started their relationship. They lived together for a year before Leo's death, a close monogamous bond. In addition to their sexual orientation, the two shared another common interest. They discovered they were both dedicated distance runners. Together they would run five, ten miles a day through the streets and parks of the city before work in the morning. Often they ran side by side in 10-kilometer and marathon races sponsored by the city. They were both in excellent condition as far as anyone could tell. Both had steady jobs. They were the envy of their gay community. Then one night just after they had sex, they were lying in bed and Leo told Sarko he had AIDS and knew he was going to die.

Q: What did you say?

A: I said, Leo, you look fine. You run fine. But he said he knew what would happen. He felt bad inside. We stayed awake all night. We cried together and I held his hand. He talked about how he was going to die.

Q: Did you have sex after that?

A: Yes, but I used a condom so I wouldn't get AIDS, too.

Q: What did he want you to do?

A: He wanted me to contact a secret organization, The Black Mask, where people with AIDS, if they want to die, they can call this organization and they will help you die. He said they operate a big business in New York and San Francisco going around killing people. Leo wanted to pay them five thousand dollars to kill him, but I didn't know how to contact the people.

Q: So then what did he say?

A: Then he asked me if I would help him do it, if I would help him strangle himself.

Q: What did you say to that?

A: I said, oh God, no, I couldn't do that. He offered me his ATM card and gave me the password to get the money out; he wanted to give me his gold rings, even his car. But I said no, I didn't know how to drive anyway.

Q: Did he finally persuade you to help him?

A: He knew how to get to me. He looked at me and said, "Steve, you don't want me to go through what your friend Eddie went through, do you?"

Sarko agreed to help Leo die. They went through another night during which they both got down on their knees and prayed together. Leo told Sarko what to do, and Sarko followed his instructions. Leo lay on the bed facedown with his hands clasped behind his back. Sarko tied Leo's hands with a belt that Sarko took from his own trousers.

Q: What did he ask you to do then?

A: He asked me to leave him like that with his hands tied behind his back, so I did. I told him I loved him, that's why I was doing it. I went into the other room. I was real tired, because we hadn't slept for two nights. I went to sleep, and when I got up and went in, he was dead. But I didn't kill him.

Up to this point, you have hardly noticed the nondescript-looking D.A., Jack Kornbluth. Short in stature, with thick glasses and thin graying hair, he has asked all his questions so far from his seat at counsel table, never raising his deep voice. You haven't even heard him make an objection. Now for the first time he gets up from his chair, moves to the podium, and glares at the defendant.

Q: Did you call the police?

A: No.

Q: Did you take care of the body, the body of your best friend?

A: No, I didn't.

Q: In fact you went into the kitchen and had a drink, didn't you?

A: Yes.

Q: And you left right away, didn't you, just left him there like that.

A: I was scared.

Q: Scared of what? You hadn't done anything wrong, had you?

A: I was scared of all the implications.

Q: You weren't too scared to take his ATM card and go down to the bank and withdraw two hundred dollars. You weren't so scared you couldn't do that, were you?

A: No.

Q: Did you do that?

A: Yes, he wanted me to.

Q: You took the gold rings?

A: Yes. He gave them to me.

Q: Tell us the truth. Isn't it a fact you killed him because you were mad at him?

A: Mad at him? God, no. I loved him. No.

Q: Come on, Mr. Sarko, level with us, weren't you mad at him because he didn't tell you he had AIDS until after you had sex with him? Didn't that make you mad?

A: Oh, no, no, no, you've got it all wrong. That wasn't it. Not that at all.

Sarko is beginning to break. The D.A. just stands and looks at him for a long time.

Q: Come on, Steve. Why don't you tell us the truth. Why don't you level with this jury. You'll feel better if you open up.

A: I didn't kill him. I swear it.

Q: All right. Then tell us how he died.

A: I told you.

Q: With his hands behind his back? Come on.

A: He wanted me to tie his neck up. But I wouldn't do that.

Q: How did he want you to tie his neck up?

A: He had this deal on his neck.

Q: What kind of deal?

A: A sash.

Q: What sash?

A: Like off a robe.

Q: He had that on his neck?

A: He had it around his neck, and he wanted me to tie that to his wrists so he could choke himself, but I wouldn't do that.

Q: So you just tied his hands?

A: Right. I just tied his hands and I left him alone with that deal around his neck. He said just to go and leave him, and I went into the living room. And I closed the door. I went to sleep, and when I went back in there he was dead.

Q: Just like that?

A: Yes.

Q: Steve—

A: I swear—

Q: Come on, Steve. A man just doesn't die from having his hands tied behind his back. You don't expect this jury to believe that?

A: I didn't kill him.

Q: How did these marks get on his neck?

Sarko looks down. He is shaking his head.

Q: How did the marks get on his neck, Mr. Sarko?

A: Well . . .

Sarko is visibly shaken.

Q: Steve, I know you want to open up. You're going to feel a lot better if you tell us the truth. For his sake, for your own soul, just tell us what happened in that bedroom.

A: Well . . . I didn't want to . . .

Q: Go ahead, let it out. Don't make his death a lie. You want to tell us.

A: When his hands were tied, I tied the sash on . . .

Q: See now. That's better. Now you're starting to tell us the truth—

A: I tied his hands like this, with the sash onto it.

Q: Okay. It's around his neck. Then you tied the sash to his hands, right?

A: Yes. That's what he asked me to do.

Q: What was he doing?

Sarko's sketch showing how Leo Melnik was tied.

A: Doing? He was trying to choke himself.

Q: And you let him do it?

A: I was scared. I didn't want him to go through what Eddie went through.

The D.A. asks Sarko to step to the board and draw a sketch showing how Melnik was tied up. Sarko is nervous. His hand is shaking. But he is a fair artist. When he is finished the sketch shows the feet also tied to the wrists.

Q: Now you're being truthful. Tied his feet, too?

A: Yes.

Q: You feel better now?

A: Yes.

Q: But you still haven't told us everything, have you?

A: What do you mean?

Q: I mean: he needed some help to die, didn't he?

A: I helped him.

Q: How did you help him?

A: I tied him.

Q: I know you tied him. Did you hold him?

A: What?

Q: Did you hold him after he was tied?

A: I just held his body.

Q: You held it?

A: Yeah. To keep from falling off the bed. He said, "Please hold me so I can do it."

Q: Did he choke?

A: Yes, sir, he choked.

Sarko is crying openly now, no longer trying to hold back the tears. His body is shaking, as if something deep inside is being forced out. You put your fingers to your eyes and they feel wet. You look at the other jurors. Some are crying too. Even the judge looks on the verge of tears.

D.A.: Go ahead, let it out, Steve, let it out.

A: I didn't do this . . . I didn't do this . . . for his money, or rings. I swear . . .

You can't make out all the words through the sobbing.

Q: Go ahead.

A: He was bucking. I had to put my hand on his back to hold him down.

Q: You were there all the time?

A: Yes. Standing beside him.

Q: You didn't choke him with your hands?

A: No! No! He was doing that himself . . .

Q: Never pulled on the sash?

A: Oh, no . . .

Q: Just enough weight on his back with your hand?

A: Yeah . . .

Q: Until it started to choke him?

A: Yes . . . Then he kicked one last time . . . the belt broke . . . and that . . . that was it . . .

Q: He was gone?

A: Yes.

Sarko leans back, exhausted. The judge hands him another tissue from the bench. There is a long silence. Finally the crying stops.

"We're in recess," the judge says.

———

Possible verdicts:
1. Guilty of first degree murder
2. Guilty of second degree murder
3. Guilty of voluntary manslaughter
4. Guilty of involuntary manslaughter
5. Guilty of assisting a suicide
6. Not guilty

WHAT IS YOUR VERDICT?

[Before choosing your verdict, see Jury Instructions 1–3, 5–13, 19, 20, starting on page 197.]

QUESTIONS AND ANALYSIS

Q1. Do jurors have the right to allow their sympathy or pity for a defendant to influence their verdict?

Q2. What is the biggest mistake the defendant made as a witness?

Q3. What well-known tactic of cross-examination did the D.A. use effectively on the defendant?

Q4. Did the defendant have a motive to murder Melnik?

Q5. If you were the defense attorney for Stephen Sarko would you want men or women on your jury, or would it make any difference, assuming all other factors are equal?

Q6. After leaving the body in the apartment, Sarko did one thing that placed him in a particularly bad light with the jury. What was it?

Q7. In his cross-examination of Sarko, the prosecutor made a number of statements imploring Sarko to tell the truth. Should defense counsel have objected? If so, on what grounds?

A1. This is the type of case in which jurors may feel pity or sympathy for the defendant. But jurors must not allow themselves to be influenced by such emotions. Their duty is to determine the facts and to apply the law to those facts. They must not be swayed by mere sentiment, conjecture, sympathy, passion, prejudice, or public opinion. In reality, however, sympathy often does influence verdicts.

A2. The defendant's biggest mistake as a witness was to lie to the jury in his direct examination. He lied when he testified on direct examination that he merely tied Melnik's hands behind his back. He thereby lost some of the sympathy jurors may have felt for him. Jurors are instructed that a witness who willfully lies in one material part of his testimony is to be distrusted in others. Not until he broke down under the D.A.'s cross-examination did the truth finally come out.

A3. The D.A. used one of the oldest devices in history to persuade Sarko to tell the truth. It can be summed up in several ways: confession is good for the soul; you'll feel better if you tell the truth; the truth will set you free. The confessional of the Catholic Church, and the psychiatrist's couch, are examples of the same theory. It doesn't often work in the public setting of the courtroom, but it did this time.

A4. Did Sarko have a motive to kill? Melnik did not tell Sarko he had AIDS until after they had sex together. It would be reasonable for Sarko to be very upset by this, and thereby have a motive to kill Melnik. Of course, Sarko denied such thoughts.

A5. Defense attorneys differ on whether to seek male or female jurors in a trial against a male homosexual, or whether it even makes any difference. Most attorneys, however, tend to favor women jurors, because women are considered more tolerant of gay men than are straight men.

A6. After leaving the body in the apartment, which was a bad move by itself, Sarko went to the bank and drew out $200 on Melnik's ATM card. This act greatly damaged his cause with the jurors. They saw it as a particularly cynical act of greed, lacking in remorse, and supporting the element of malice.

A7. Yes, defense counsel should have objected to the prosecutor's statements imploring Sarko to tell the truth on the grounds that they were not questions at all. Cross-examination should be limited to questions without comments by the examiner. Such statements as "You'll feel better if you open up" and "Come on, Steve, why don't you tell us the truth" proved to be effective with the jury, but it was improper cross-examination and most judges would have sustained an objection. Fortunately for him, the prosecutor got away with it here.

VERDICT

GUILTY OF MURDER IN THE SECOND DEGREE

The defense had high hopes for a verdict of Assisting a Suicide, but this case was won by the effective cross-examination of the District Attorney. His unique posture as a father-confessor trying to help the defendant gained the trust of the jury. Sarko's lies on direct examination hurt the defense.

(Sentence: Fifteen years to life in prison)

ELISE WARNER, GUARDIAN FOR ROSA MOSCINI, v. GUNTHER MARX, M.D.

You are juror number eight, and for the first time since you have been called to jury duty you have been assigned to a civil case. You will soon find out that civil cases can be even more dramatic than criminal cases.

"I wish to introduce the parties to this action," the judge, a good-looking woman in her late thirties, says to the jury. "This is the plaintiff, Mrs. Elise Warner."

Mrs. Warner stands, biting her lips. She is a gray-haired woman of about sixty-five. She seems frightened, overwhelmed by the courtroom scene. When Mrs. Warner sits down, her attorney, Josephine Keegan, touches her arm as if to reassure her client.

The defendant, Dr. Gunther Marx, then rises when the judge introduces him. He is balding, with a Vandyke beard, and looks very uncomfortable. You notice that he avoids looking at Mrs. Warner except for occasional stealthy glances.

"The question the court must decide," the judge says, "is whether a feeding tube that now keeps Rosa Moscini, age ninety-two, alive, should be removed at her daughter's request so that Mrs. Moscini may be allowed to die. The daughter is the plaintiff in this action, Elise Warner.

"Although such cases are generally tried by the judge alone, the parties have requested a jury to decide certain questions of fact. Your answers will guide the court in making its final decision."

You shift nervously in your seat. The juror next to you whispers, "Oh, my God!" It never occurred to you that in a civil trial you would have to decide whether a woman should live or die.

The portly man on the stand is Peter Warner, the plaintiff's first witness. He testifies he is forty-three years old and lives with his wife and four children in San Francisco. His mother, Elise Warner, is sixty-five years old; his grandmother, Rosa Moscini, is ninety-two.

The plaintiff's attorney, Josephine Keegan, is conducting the direct examination:

Q: You are the only grandson of Rosa Moscini?

A: Yes.

Q: And the only son of Elise Warner, Mrs. Moscini's daughter, the plaintiff in this action?

A: That's correct.

Q: You saw your grandmother often?

A: Oh, yes, ever since I can remember. When I was growing up I used to spend summers at her house in Santa Monica.

Q: You had many talks?

A: Yes.

Q: Based on your knowledge of your grandmother, do you have an opinion as to whether she would want to be kept alive in a coma the way she is now?

Dr. Marx's attorney, Elizabeth Rico, a small, wiry woman, jumps to her feet.

"Objection! Calls for speculation."

"Sustained," the judge says. "Counsel, you'll have to lay a better foundation before I will allow the witness to give such an opinion."

Keegan nods respectfully and resumes her questioning.

Q: All right, did you have a chance to observe your grandmother's attitude toward life?

A: Yes. She was full of life. Spent a lot of time giving herself to others. I can't believe she'd ever want to be lying in bed like a vegetable this way.

Q: She ever tell you that?

A: No, unfortunately the question never came up. But she was always active, going all the time.

Q: Wanted to be involved in everything?

A: That's right.

Q: I will ask you again. In your opinion would your grandmother want to be kept alive by a feeding tube in a nursing home?

"Same objection," the defense attorney says. "She never told him whether she would or not, Your Honor. How would he know? It's pure speculation."

"Objection sustained," the judge says.

This time Keegan resists the judge's ruling.

"But Your Honor, it's the only way we can show what Mrs. Moscini would want in her condition—through those who knew her, her attitude on life. She did not sign a living will instructing the family what to do if she lost her faculties; she did not sign a durable power of attorney for health care; she did not sign a directive to doctors; she did not specify what she would want in any other form except by implication in the way she lived. These circumstances go to show what she would want done."

The judge pauses. "All right," she says, "the witness may answer."

"I'll try, Your Honor," Peter Warner says. "My grandmother was very strong-willed, she took hold of life, always up early and doing things. If somebody got sick, she was the one who took care of them. If in those days there was such a thing as a living will or whatever the term is, she would have signed it. She would never have wanted to live the way she is now. And that's not an opinion, ma'am, that's a fact."

Elise Warner takes the stand. She is the guardian and conservator for her mother, Rosa Moscini. For many years after her father's death her mother lived alone with a housekeeper. When her mother reached her late eighties she began to grow senile and needed more care. She was showing signs of Alzheimer's disease. When Mrs. Warner tried to place her in a nursing home, her mother escaped in a wheelchair and had to be pursued in the street. She was moved into Mrs. Warner's home, but it was difficult because Mrs. Warner's husband was ill with cancer. Mother and daughter had minor arguments, nothing serious. They loved each other, and Mrs. Warner wanted only the best for her.

Then one day, about a year earlier during the summer of 1985, Mrs. Moscini choked on some food, causing asphyxiation. The paramedics came to the house and had to resuscitate her. Mrs. Moscini was rushed to the hospital. She suffered severe brain damage, never recovered, never regained consciousness, and has not spoken to anyone since. She is totally unable to care for her bodily needs. She was moved to a nursing home where she is fed with a tube, called a nasogastric tube, which enters through her nose, passes through the back of her throat, down her esophagus, and into her stomach. The nurses feed her fluids and nourishment in this way, since she is unable to eat or swallow anything on her own.

Mrs. Warner is crying quietly.

Q: Did you ask Dr. Marx to remove the tube?

A: Yes.

Q: What did he say?

A: He said she would die.

Q: What did you say?

A: I said, "For God's sake that's what she would want. That's what her family wants. For her own good. This is abhorrent to her."

Q: His reply?

A: He said he could not do that, because the nurses would report him.

Q: He refused?

A: Yes. He said he was terribly sorry, but his hands were tied. He said I would need a court order.

The crying is more obvious now. She asks the judge for a tissue to wipe her eyes. "Please," she says to the jury, "please, somebody, let my mother die in peace . . . she'd never want to live like this."

Q: When your mother was competent, did she ever express to you her views about being kept alive this way?

A: She hated the thought of it.

Q: Did she ever say anything specific?

A: When she was much younger, in her sixties, I remember she was part of a group of volunteers that would visit the old age home. She'd go to help them, read to them, entertain them on their birthdays. There were people there the same age she was, but she thought they were old. She told me it was terrible to live that way; she said, "I'd rather be dead than live that way."

Q: How many times did you hear her say that?

A: Several times.

Now Dr. Marx's attorney, Elizabeth Rico, takes the witness on cross-examination. She is less than five feet tall, but her voice booms out in clear, stentorian tones.

Q: You say you once heard Mrs. Moscini say she'd rather be dead than living in a nursing home?

A: Yes.

Q: How long ago was that?

A: Oh, about thirty years ago.

Q: In her whole lifetime did you ever hear her say anything else along those lines?

A: Oh, let's see, I remember once a good friend of hers had a stroke and she said she'd never want to be in that situation.

Q: How long ago was that?

A: About . . . she was about fifty then . . .

Q: About forty years ago?

A: Yes.

Q: And you never had any conversation with her as to how she wished to be cared for if she was in a comatose state?

A: She didn't believe she could ever become comatose, so the subject never came up.

Q: So your answer is no, you never had any such conversation?

A: Correct.

Rico looks at Mrs. Warner for several seconds before continuing.

Q: I know this may not seem polite, but I must ask it—it's become relevant . . .

A: Go ahead, you have your job to do.

Q: Your mother's estate: you would inherit the bulk of that upon her death, isn't that true?

A: I don't need that money. I'm very comfortable financially. I'm not interested in her money. You're not suggesting—

Q: Please, Mrs. Warner, I'm not suggesting anything. I'm just asking a question.

A: This is an insult to our family—

Q: Please just answer the question: would you be the sole inheritor of her estate?

A: Yes, but I've discussed that with her. I'll keep that money in trust for Peter's children, my grandchildren.

Q: But you would get control of it on her death?

A: Yes.

Q: And you could invade the principal of that trust if you wanted to?

A: I don't know. I really haven't thought about that.

Q: How much is it worth?

"Oh, for God's sake." She turns to the judge. "Do I have to answer, Your Honor?

Judge: I am sorry, Mrs. Warner, but you have to answer, yes.

A: I'm not sure how much it is.

Q: Would the amount of $600,000 sound about right?

A: I don't know . . . well, yes . . . Yes! My God!

Q: Thank you, that's all.

Mrs. Warner remains on the witness stand, sobbing audibly for several minutes, before she steps down.

The plaintiff rests.

Rico opens the defense case by calling Dr. Marx to the stand. Up to this time he has been seated beside his lawyer at counsel table. It is obvious from the expressions on his face so far that this trial has been a very unpleasant experience. Dr. Marx testifies he is a licensed physician with a specialty in internal medicine and cardiology. He first began to see Rosa Moscini professionally ten years ago and has been her primary physician ever since. She was competent when he first saw her for a hypothyroid condition, which still exists. Mrs. Moscini had three children. He noticed her mental status began to change with the death of her only son about seven years ago. Then a daughter, Elise Warner's sister, died, and now Elise is left as the only surviving child. As each child died, Mrs. Moscini's mental condition became worse. She suffered a cardiopulmonary arrest last year from choking on some food at home and never recovered.

Rico continues the direct examination of her client.

Q: You understand you are not being sued for money?

A: I understand that.

Q: You are in court because you are the physician in charge, and Mrs. Warner wants you to remove the tube. You refuse to do that, is that correct?

A: That's correct. I cannot do that. I respect Mrs. Warner's wishes. It troubles me to see the anguish she is going through, but I cannot do what she asks.

Q: Why not?

A: If I removed the tube, Mrs. Moscini would die. I didn't become a doctor to put my patients to death. I am not in the business of killing people. I am in the business of helping people live.

Q: Even if it is the request of her daughter and family?

A: I cannot do it.

Q: Even if Mrs. Warner is acting as her conservator, her guardian?

A: I cannot do it! It is against my principles.

Q: What principles?

A: My ethical principles, first of all. She never told me she'd want me to let her die in this situation.

Q: In all the years . . .

A: In all the years I treated her, she never expressed her views to me if it came to this.

Q: So you don't know what she'd want you to do.

A: I have no idea. I am not about to guess.

Q: You've told us about your ethical principles. What about your medical principles?

A: Look, the woman has severe damage to the brain. She may never recover. But she is not what you'd call brain-dead. It is still possible she could improve somewhat. When I have been in the room to examine her, her eyes open and sometimes appear to be tracking. When I move from one side to the other, the eyes appear to move. Whether that's reflex or not, I can't be sure. When I put the stethoscope to her chest, there's response; she appears to respond to touch.

Q: Is she in pain?

A: There is no certain medical evidence she is in pain, no.

Q: Can she talk?

A: No.

Q: Is she comatose?

A: Only partly comatose. Not completely.

Q: Does she understand anything?

A: I don't know if she comprehends anything.

Q: Is it your opinion, Doctor, that it is medically inappropriate to withdraw the feeding tube?

A: Yes, it is.

Q: Assuming you were ordered to remove the tube, would you be personally concerned about repercussions from the State Board of Medical Quality Assurance, or the AMA?

A: Yes, I would be.

Q: Your witness.

Keegan cross-examines the doctor.

Q: Dr. Marx, you have testified that you don't know what Mrs. Moscini's views are—

A: That's correct.

Q: —as to having the tube removed.

A: Correct.

Q: Doctor, suppose Mrs. Moscini signed a sworn statement, while competent, requesting that if this situation came up, she'd want the tube removed and to be allowed to die in peace, suppose—

Defense Attorney Rico: Objection, Your Honor! There is no such statement and counsel knows it! This is pure speculation.

Plaintiff's Attorney Keegan: Your Honor, this isn't a trick. Yes, I am quite aware no such document exists. But I pose this hypothetical question to enable the court to understand the doctor's state of mind.

Judge: Objection overruled. The doctor may answer.

A: If she requested it?

Q: Yes.

The doctor pauses, reflects. He shakes his head.

A: No, I still could not do it. I would not want to be involved.

Q: Why?

A: Because it's wrong, that's why. It's morally and ethically wrong! It's medically wrong!

Q: Doctor, as a licensed physician in this state, are you aware of any regulations that would subject you to disciplinary action for complying with a court order to remove the tube?

A: No, I am not.

Q: Then why . . .

A: But I remember a few years ago, two doctors in California were charged with murder for withdrawing the artificial feeding mechanism from a patient, resulting in his death.

Q: Do you know what happened to that case, Doctor?

A: Well, I'm not sure . . .

Q: Isn't it a fact those charges were dismissed?

A: That may be. But if I removed the tube, I think my professional standing would suffer.

Q: Even if the court ordered it, even if the family wanted it, even if—

A: I'm sorry. I have to live with myself.

The doctor leans back, exhausted. He looks at you. "Don't ask me to do it. I could not do it." He turns to the judge. "May I add something, Your Honor?"

Judge: Go ahead.

A: I don't know of any other doctor who would do it, either.

Q: Have you asked?

A: I have asked. I have talked to my colleagues. I put a notice on the bulletin board. I have not found anyone who would do it.

As the doctor leaves the witness stand, the juror in front of you stands up. "Your Honor," she says, "I have a request. Is it possible for the jury to visit the nursing home to see Mrs. Moscini for ourselves?"

The judge seems taken aback by the request. She summons the attorneys to the side bar for a conference outside of your hearing. Then she announces to the jury that counsel agree the request is reasonable under the circumstances; the jury will be taken by bus to the nursing home tomorrow provided the medical staff at the nursing home can assure the judge that the visit will present no additional danger to the patient. Court is adjourned.

In the courtroom next morning the judge instructs the jurors on their conduct at the nursing home. No testimony will be taken. The visit is to observe Rosa Moscini only. There must be no discussion of her condition among jurors.

When the jury bus pulls up to the nursing home you are confronted with a strange scene. As you disembark, a group of about twenty-five persons carrying picket signs begins to march in a circle near the entrance. "Don't pay any attention," the judge shouts. You try to avert your eyes, but you cannot help seeing a large sign that says LET ROSA MOSCINI LIVE, and another THOU SHALT NOT KILL.

As you enter, the pickets are chanting: "Let Rosa live! Let Rosa live!" The judge and her bailiff hurry all of you inside. As soon as the doors close behind you, the judge gathers the jurors around her in the reception room.

"What you have just seen and heard must be stricken from your minds," she says. "Disregard it. It is not evidence in this case. Treat it as though it never happened."

In the room occupied by Rosa Moscini you and the other jurors gather around her bed in a semicircle. You see an emaciated woman lying in bed, with a small tube from each nostril attached to a feeding apparatus. Her eyes are open, but you cannot tell if she sees anything. At times her eyes appear to track a moving person. The jurors stand silently. The only sounds are some moans and grunts coming from Rosa Moscini's mouth. Once or twice she belches; she chews. One of the jurors, the woman who requested the visit, goes up to her and calls out her name, but there is no response—just a blank stare. Now you go up to her. You ask the nurse if it is all right to hold Mrs. Moscini's hand, and the nurse nods approval. You take her hand in yours. You squeeze it slightly. No response. You are near tears. The hand is warm, but it drops like a dead thing.

After a while the judge signals it is time to leave. "We'll go out the back way," she says, "to avoid the demonstrators. Court resumes at one P.M."

When court resumes after lunch, the plaintiff's attorney Keegan calls one final witness in rebuttal, Dr. Robert Sugarman. He testifies he is the consulting neurologist in the case.

Q: You were contacted by Dr. Marx to examine Rosa Moscini?

A: Yes.

Q: Dr. Marx is an expert in cardiology, pertaining to the heart?

A: That's right.

Q: So he contacted you because you are an expert in neurology, pertaining to the brain?

A: Yes.

Dr. Sugarman testifies he has examined Mrs. Moscini on several occasions, the last time being this morning before the jury arrived at the nursing home. He says there has been no significant change in her condition over the past year.

Q: Is she still in a coma?

A: Some people call it a coma. I call it a vegetative state.

Q: Which means . . . ?

A: It means her bodily functions are all going on. The heart is going. The blood is pumping. But mentally she is not functioning.

Q: Can you explain, Doctor?

A: The brain is divided into two basic parts, the brain stem and the cerebral cortex. The brain stem is the core of the brain; it connects the brain to the spinal cord and to the rest of the nervous system.

Q: Is it functioning in Rosa Moscini, Doctor?

A: At the most primitive level, yes.

Q: What about the cerebral cortex?

A: The cerebral cortex is not functioning. This is the so-called gray matter, the lumpy-looking stuff everybody thinks of as the brain. The jury may have seen Mrs. Moscini react in some way, but if she did it was as reflex, not voluntary. All voluntary movement originates in the cortex. Thinking, understanding language—they are functions of the cortex—

Q: Did you see any signs of cortical functions?

A: No, she's lost those functions.

Q: Permanently?

"Yes." The doctor pauses. He looks at the jury. "Yes. Permanently."

[Before you answer the following questions, see Jury Instructions 2, 21, 22, starting on page 197.]

In the Superior Court
State of California

ELISE WARNER,

on behalf of ROSA MOSCINI

v.

GUNTHER MARX, M.D.

Answers to Special Interrogatories

1. Would Mrs. Moscini want the feeding tube removed, knowing she would then die?

                                YES   NO
                                  (Circle one)

2. If it is not possible to ascertain what Mrs. Moscini's choice would be, is it still in her best interest to remove the tube?

                                YES   NO
                                  (Circle one)

3. Is Mrs. Warner's request to have the tube removed made:

                      a) In the best interest of her mother?
                                    OR
                      b) For her own financial gain?
                              (Circle one)

DATE:_____   _____
                                      Presiding Juror

QUESTIONS AND ANALYSIS

Q1. In this tour of duty as a juror, this was your first civil case. What is the difference in the burden of proof required in a civil case compared to a criminal case?

Q2. In a right-to-die case such as the one you just heard, where the final decision means life or death, should the plaintiff's burden of proving that the patient should be allowed to die be greater than in the usual civil case?

Q3. During the trial a juror stood up and asked for more evidence—specifically, to visit and observe the patient, Rosa Moscini. Should such requests be allowed by the court?

Q4. In the Moscini trial, both attorneys as well as the judge were women. Do you find that scenario unusual?

Q5. The doctor testified that removing the tube and allowing Mrs. Moscini to die would be medically and ethically wrong. Should this opinion of the doctor's be a determining factor in the final decision?

———

A1. In the normal civil trial, the plaintiff has the burden of proving her or his case by a preponderance of the evidence. This means the evidence in favor of the plaintiff must have more convincing force, however slight, than the evidence opposed to it. The civil plaintiff has no burden of proof beyond a reasonable doubt. This burden is much lighter than the burden required in a criminal case, in which the state must prove its case beyond any reasonable doubt and to a moral certainty.

A2.   There is a strong current of opinion that because of the conse-
        quences involved, the burden of proof in right-to-die cases should
        be greater than in the usual civil trial. In 1990 the United States
        Supreme Court approved a burden of proof for such cases heavier
        than the usual preponderance of the evidence. In the case of *Cruzan
        v. Missouri Department of Health*, the Supreme Court held that a state
        could require plaintiffs to prove a comatose patient's wish to die by
        clear and convincing evidence. In the context of our case, "clear and
        convincing" means the proof must persuade the trier of fact that the
        patient held a firm and settled commitment to withdrawing the
        feeding tube.

A3.   Judges differ on whether to allow jurors to ask questions or request
        more evidence. Generally judges frown on the practice because of
        the danger of opening the door to a barrage of questions by jurors,
        thereby removing control of the case from the attorneys. Some
        judges, without encouraging it, will allow jurors to submit written
        questions, which the judge will consider in conference with coun-
        sel. After all, the goal of the court is a fair trial, and if the juror's
        question or request helps further that goal, it should at least be
        considered.

A4.   The scenario in which both attorneys and the judge are women is no
        longer unusual. One of the most remarkable changes in jury trials,
        in fact in the entire legal system, over the past quarter century has
        been the inclusion of women as attorneys and judges. Twenty-five
        years ago this scene would have been most unusual. In fact there
        was also a time when women were not even allowed on the jury. In
        California, for example, prior to 1917 a jury was defined as "a body
        of men," and women were not qualified for jury service. A state law
        was passed in 1917 that expressly extended this right to women.
        The federal courts, however, did not allow women jurors until 1919.

A5.   Under existing law, the doctor's medical and ethical opinion should
        not be a determining factor in the court's final life-or-death decision.
        What is involved here is the constitutional right of privacy: the right
        of the individual to refuse medical treatment. This right takes prece-

dence over the doctor's medical and ethical beliefs and must not be abridged. Her wish is the determining factor. In our case, of course, the court was faced with the factual question of what her wish was, since she was in a comatose state and could not express it to the court.

VERDICT

VERDICT FOR THE PLAINTIFF

The Moscini case was actually tried before a judge alone, but because of widespread interest in the subject we have presented it as a jury trial.

The judge found in the plaintiff's favor; that there was sufficient evidence Mrs. Moscini would have wanted the tube removed, that it was in her best interest to do so, and that Mrs. Warner was motivated by the best interests of her mother rather than financial gain. The judge ordered the doctor to grant Mrs. Warner's request, but the doctor refused on the grounds it was against his personal ethics. The judge tried to find another doctor in the county who would remove the tube but was told all took the same position. Mrs. Moscini was moved to another county, where she died before the tube was ever removed.

This case illustrates the difficult, indeed agonizing, questions presented by the increasing power of modern science to keep the human body alive by artificial means.

STATE *v.* CARVALHO

In March 1990 Judge Ehrenfreund was invited, along with a team of American lawyers, to Lisbon by the new democratic government of Portugal. They had been asked to demonstrate the American jury system through a mock criminal trial. Coauthor Lawrence Treat accompanied him and attended the trial as an observer.

The major difference between American jury trials and those elsewhere is in the role of the judge and the responsibility placed upon the jury. In England, for example, the judge sums up the case for the jury as he or she sees it. Of course, the judge is supposed to be objective. However, he or she has the power to give the jurors a lead, a suggestion, as to which way to go. The jurors, seeing the judge as the embodiment of the law, will usually follow that lead. In Portugal and other European countries judges and jurors generally sit together, confer together, decide together in a joint effort unheard of in America. For the most part, judges in foreign jury trials get the verdicts they want.

Not so in America. Our judge and jury are completely separate and have distinct roles. The judge decides the law; the jury decides the facts. Our judges rarely comment on the evidence—it is considered bad form to do so. The American judge must always be on guard not to show the slightest leaning one way or another. We place trust in the jury to do the right thing, and in this respect our system is unique.

When Judge Ehrenfreund asked the Portuguese what kind of trial they wished to see, they requested a scenario in which a wife, allegedly battered by her husband, finally shoots and kills him. English-speaking jurors were chosen from the Lisbon community.

You are juror number nine, and you are nervous because many people in your country of Portugal, as well as in other countries, are watching what the jury does in this case. The room is a large, stark chamber with thick, sturdy columns. Once part of a prison, with barred windows as a grim reminder of its past, now it is a courtroom jammed with several hundred lawyers, judges, and scholars from many lands come to see their first American jury trial.

The accused is Maria Carvalho, a pale, harmless-looking woman, slumped beside her attorney. The charge is murder.

"You may feel some sympathy for Maria," prosecutor Maurice Sands says in his opening statement. "But sympathy has no part in this case. Do not let it sway you. She is a murderess and must pay the price for her deed."

Maria Carvalho's attorney, Philip Bourne, stands behind her with one hand on her shoulder as he makes his opening statement.

"Maria shot her husband because there was no other way out for her. She shot him out of fear he would beat her again, as he had done so many times in the past."

You look at Maria Carvalho. The tears are already beginning to form in her eyes.

The first witness for the prosecution is Ilde Diaz, next-door neighbor to Armando and Maria Carvalho and their two-year-old daughter in Lisbon's Alfama district. She testifies that on the morning of January 3, 1990, at about 5:00 A.M., she heard three shots coming from the direction of the Carvalho apartment. She was lying awake in bed at the time, and after hearing the shots she dressed and looked out in the hallway. She noticed the Carvalhos' front door open. She rang the bell, knocked several times, announced her presence and finally, when no one responded, she went inside. There she saw the body of Armando Carvalho lying faceup on the sofa. He wore only a bathrobe, and she could see a considerable amount of blood in the area of his chest and shoulders. He appeared to be dead, so she immediately called the police.

The prosecutor, Maurice Sands, asks her about the shots.

Q: You are sure you heard three shots?

A: Yes, quite sure.

Q: Tell us how they were spaced as to the time between each shot.

A: The first two came in rapid succession, one right after another, boom-boom. The third came a bit later.

Q: How much later?

A: That's hard to say.

"I will ask you to try to remember in this way," Sands says. He looks up at the big clock on the wall. "I am looking at the clock. Imagine you are in your bed at the time of the shots. When I say 'Now!' think of that as the second shot. Then think to yourself the time that passed, and say 'Now' when you heard the third shot."

The audience is hushed. Along with everyone else, you and the other jurors watch the red second hand as it goes around. When it reaches "12," the prosecutor shouts, "Now!" The witness has her eyes closed. One second, two, three, four, five, six—"Now!" she says.

"Thank you, Mrs. Diaz. Your Honor, may the record show six seconds passed between the two 'Nows'?"

Judge: The record may so show.

The witness also testifies that during a casual conversation with the victim about a month before the shooting, he mentioned that he had a fight with his wife the night before and that he believed his wife was mentally ill and might try to kill him someday. She couldn't tell if he was serious. She asked him if he wanted to report his wife to the police, and he insisted that he did not.

Under cross-examination the witness testifies she often heard arguments between the couple, especially during the month before the shooting. She could hear the loud voice of Mr. Carvalho and at times the screaming of the defendant. She could never make out the words. On the evening before the shooting she heard another such argument. This time she also heard the sound of breaking glass and of furniture falling over.

It is Sands's turn to question.

Q: What time was it when you heard this argument?

A: About ten P.M.

Q: Did you hear anything sounding like an argument after that?

A: No.

Q: Before the shots were fired about five A.M., did you hear any argument, anything at all?

A: No, nothing.

Q: You said you often heard arguments between the couple. Ever see the defendant, Mrs. Carvalho, after one of these arguments?

A: Oh yes, many times.

Q: Ever see any marks on her body?

A: No.

Q: Black eyes, bruises, anything like that?

A: No, I never did.

Sands is finished with the witness, but Bourne still has a question.

Q: How did she look after these arguments?

A: Very depressed.

Q: Frightened?

Sands: Objection! Calls for a conclusion.

Judge: Overruled. You may answer.

A: You might say she looked scared, yes.

Bourne: Thank you.

Officer Miguel Tavares was the first police officer on the scene. He testifies he found the victim lying on his back on the sofa clothed only in a robe. The deceased had visible wounds to his right hand, left shoulder, and chest. The sofa where the victim was lying was soaked with blood. The room had a bed and a sofa. After the body was removed, he searched the apartment with other members of the homicide squad. He found no weapons. There was one spent bullet embedded in the wall above the sofa where the body was discovered, about five feet above the floor. Except for the blood on the sofa, he found no other traces of blood. Several bottles of alcohol including wine, vodka, and brandy stood open on the table. In the dining room the officer noted an overturned chair and what appeared to be pieces of a smashed glass. He also found a small amount of cocaine and items used for sniffing it.

The prosecution next calls its forensic pathologist, Dr. Duarte Vasconcelos. He performed the autopsy and says the gunshot wound to the chest was the principal cause of death. The doctor testifies he found a through-and-through bullet wound to the right hand, entering the palm just under the index finger and exiting the back of the hand. The palm of the right hand showed tattooing and powder burns, indicating the bullet was fired at close range. A second bullet struck the left shoulder and was still lodged in the back behind the shoulder. The third shot was also a through-and-through wound, entering just above the breastbone at about a forty-five-degree angle to the chest. He explains he was able to determine the path of entry and exit from careful examination of the wounds. The doctor draws the diagram below with the body in a horizontal position to show how the bullet entered the chest and exited the back.

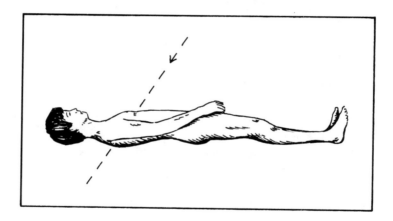

He found no tattooing or powder burns in the wounds to the shoulder or chest, indicating those shots were fired at a greater distance than the shot to the hand, at least four feet from the body. There were small amounts of cocaine and alcohol found in the blood and urine. The blood alcohol level was .18 percent, well above the amount at which an individual is considered too intoxicated to drive a car.

Bourne takes the doctor on cross-examination.

Q: Any way to tell in which order the three shots were fired, Doctor?

A: No way I can say that.

Q: You testified the shot to the hand occurred at close range. How close?

A: One can't say exactly. But within a foot or so.

Q: Would that be consistent with the victim's trying to strike Maria with that hand when the shot was fired?

Sands: Objection! Beyond his expertise.

Judge: Sustained.

Q: Doctor, I notice you drew your diagram with the body lying down. Is it your testimony the body was in that position when the shot was fired?

A: I cannot testify to that, no. I can only say this is the angle at which the fatal bullet entered the body. I'm afraid I assumed he was in that position because the body was found on the sofa, lying down, with blood on the blanket.

Q: So that position is just an assumption.

A: Yes, from what I was told by the police.

Q: Thank you, Doctor. By the way, how tall was Mr. Carvalho?

A: Let me check my notes . . . ah, yes, he measured five feet eleven inches.

Q: And weight?

A: 176 pounds.

Bourne: Your Honor, I will ask my client to stand so the jurors may observe her approximate height and weight.

Maria Carvalho stands up, and you look at her size. She is only about five feet three inches tall, about 120 pounds in weight.

The prosecution calls another neighbor to the stand. Luis Caetano testifies he lived in the apartment directly opposite the Carvalhos'. He knew them both, especially Maria, since they had grown up in the same neighborhood of Lisbon. He recalls having a conversation with Maria on the day before Christmas 1989. She told him she feared she would have to kill her husband because of his violence to her. She also told him her husband had beaten her on several occasions during the last three years, to the point where she was considering leaving home with their child.

Sands pauses before resuming direct examination.

Q: You would see her often?

A: Yes.

Q: Ever see any effects of a beating—marks, bruises, anything like that?

A: No, I never did.

Q: Did you ask her about that?

A: Yes.

Q: And what was her response?

A: She said her husband was always careful to hit her only on the torso, or ribs, so it would not show.

As is his habit, Bourne wastes no time on cross-examination.

Q: You knew Maria well?

A: Yes.

Q: You consider her honest, truthful?

A: Of course.

"Thank you."

The next witness, Philippe Castro, identifies himself as a close friend of the deceased. He says that about two days after Christmas 1989 he went to dinner with the deceased. During the dinner Carvalho stated several times he feared his wife was going to kill him.

Under cross-examination the witness admits he has been convicted of two prior felonies: credit card fraud in 1986, and vehicular manslaughter in 1962.

The judge tells you that you may take his prior felony conviction into consideration in judging his credibility, but it doesn't necessarily mean he is lying.

The final witness for the prosecution is a woman who is brought in under guard. Her name is Teresa Salazar, and she testifies she is currently being detained at the Lisbon detention facility for women, awaiting trial on a charge of selling narcotics. She says that on the morning of January 5, 1990, she was having breakfast with another inmate, Maria Carvalho, at the jail. During the course of the conversation Maria told her she was glad she killed her husband, that he treated her badly, and that she knew for some time she would have to kill him to get away from him. The witness further testifies the defendant also told her that if she got out she would not hesitate to harm any member of her husband's family if they tried to take her child away from her. The witness says she made some notes of the conversation immediately afterwards, because she knew they would be important to the police, but the piece of paper was confiscated before the trial during a routine search of jail lockers.

Bourne takes the witness on cross-examination:

Q: Did the police tell you it might be better for you in your own case if you testified for the prosecution here?

A: No.

Q: No promises of benefit of any kind?

A: No.

Q: What did they tell you?

A: They asked me if I would cooperate, and I said I would.

Q: Why?

A: Well . . . so the truth would come out.

Q: And you hoped that by telling what you call the truth you might get a break from the police?

A: No, they made no promises. They even said they couldn't make any promises.

Q: Didn't they say they would tell your judge you cooperated?

A: Well . . . yes, but no promises of leniency.

Q: But you hope you will get a break, that the judge will go easier on you if he knows you helped the police?

A: Well . . .

Q: Well what?

A: Well, of course, if I can get a better deal for myself, fine, I don't want to go to prison.

"Thank you, that's all."

The prosecution rests.

Bourne begins the defense's case by calling the defendant's mother, Eliana Viriato. She testifies that on the morning of January 3, 1990, about 5:15 A.M., she received a phone call from her daughter, who was crying; she asked her parents to come pick her up right away. Mrs. Viriato testifies she and her husband drove to the apartment, where Maria was waiting outside with her child. She hysterically told her parents she just shot her husband, and they drove her to the police station, where she turned herself in.

Sands cross-examines in a kindly manner:

Q: Did she have the gun with her?

A: No, we didn't see any. And we didn't ask her about it.

Q: Did she seem to be in possession of all her faculties?

A: Well, she kept crying all the time.

Q: But did she seem to know what she was doing, what she was saying?

A: Yes.

Now a psychiatrist, Dr. Fritz Mannheim, takes the stand. He has impressive credentials. He testifies that at the request of Mr. Bourne he interviewed Maria five times in the Lisbon jail after her arrest. He directed a psychologist to give her the standard psychological tests. He says he found no major organic deficiency, but she was suffering from major depression resulting from her husband's treatment of her; that at the time of the shooting she was suicidal and saw no hope for herself or her child. He says he tried to get her to tell him what happened, but the events were unclear in her mind. This failure to recall, the doctor says, is consistent with a woman suffering from such a mental illness; she wants to leave such an experience behind and not relive it in any way, either with her psychiatrist or in the courtroom. The doctor testifies Maria was suffering from "battered woman's syndrome," resulting from a cycle of emotional and physical abuse by her husband, from which she could see no options for escape.

Sands begins questioning, with a note of cynicism in his voice:

Q: Doctor, do you consider the defendant as your client?

A: Oh, no, I was simply asked to evaluate her for the court.

Q: Who is paying you for your services?

A: Mr. Bourne is taking care of that.

Q: How much are you being paid?

"Well . . ." He begins to speak, then turns to the judge. "Do I have to answer that, Your Honor?"

Judge: You do, sir.

A: One hundred fifty an hour for services out of court and . . .

Q: And more if you testify?

A: Yes. Two hundred fifty an hour as a witness in court.

Q: And if your opinion is adverse to the defense, you do not testify?

A: I testify if I am called as a witness.

Q: And it's to your advantage to testify?

A: I consider your line of questioning insulting, sir.

Q: By the way, Doctor, is there any scientifically verifiable test to determine mental illness?

A: Well, no.

Q: It's a matter of subjective determination, isn't that true?

A: One may say that.

Q: And there is no scientifically verifiable test to determine what Maria Carvalho was thinking on the morning of January 3, 1990?

A: That is true.

Q: And isn't it also true that reasonable psychiatrists, qualified experts such as yourself, might disagree as to such a diagnosis?

A: That is also true, yes.

Bourne gets up immediately for redirect examination.

Q: Doctor, based on all your training and experience, do you have an opinion as to why Maria shot her husband?

A: I do.

Q: Tell the jury, please.

A: In my opinion she believed she had to shoot him in order to protect herself and her child from further abuse.

The next witness for the defense is a criminologist from the Lisbon Police Department, who testifies he took blood and urine samples from the defendant immediately following her arrest on January 3, 1990, and found no evidence of alcohol or cocaine in her body.

A detention officer who works in the women's detention facility testifies that she inspected the items seized in the search of Teresa Salazar's locker and found no notes of a conversation with the defendant.

Defense attorney Bourne casually announces that Maria Carvalho will be his next witness. You feel relieved. You wanted to hear her testify. Now you will. She seems a pathetic little figure as she walks slowly to the stand, on the verge of tears even before the first question is asked. She testifies she and Armando were very much in love when they married five years ago. They both had good jobs and looked forward to a happy life. When their child was born, another dream was fulfilled. But then Armando changed, started drinking and using cocaine. He became abusive to her, not so much physically as emotionally, always putting her down, humiliating her, screaming at her, threatening her with violence in front of their little girl. At times, although not often, he would actually beat her with his fists. He never struck her in the face. After each bout of violence he would be remorseful and they would reconcile.

This went on for the last year and a half of their marriage and seemed to get worse around Christmas 1989. She became quite depressed, often lost her drive to get up in the morning, felt there was no way out and thought of killing herself. On the night of January 2, 1990, they had another bitter argument. She wanted him to stop using cocaine, and he resented her telling him how to live his life. He punched her in the shoulder, and she finally went to bed crying while he stood over her and threatened to hit her if she didn't stop acting like a child. The night passed. He slept on the sofa, the one on which he was found dead. She awoke while it was still dark. She was very depressed and thought of killing herself. She lay back thinking how she would do it. She remembered his gun was in the drawer next to the bed. After that, she cannot recall. She knows she must have shot him from what others told her, but she has no recollection how it happened.

Sands drops his sympathetic demeanor as he begins cross-examining.

Q: Did you have to shoot to defend yourself?

A: I don't know. I can't remember.

Q: Did he attack you that morning?

A: I can't say.

Q: You say you were very depressed and suicidal. Did you ever seek counseling or any medical assistance for your condition?

A: No, I didn't think it could help.

Q: It didn't occur to you that that might be an alternative to killing your husband?

"Objection!"

"Sustained."

Q: Did you ever report any of these beatings to the police?

A: No. What good would that do?

Q: Did you have a chance to get away?

A: Well . . . yes . . . but . . .

Q: You could have gone to the police?

A: Yes.

Q: You could have gone to neighbors? to your parents?

A: No, I really couldn't . . . they had no room . . .

Q: Did you ever try any of these things?

A: I couldn't! I couldn't! I felt so . . . so trapped . . . [she is sobbing now] I can't explain . . .

Q: No, I guess you can't explain. Thank you, ma'am. No further questions.

Bourne recalls Officer Tavares to the stand. He was the officer who made the search of the apartment.

Q: Officer, you testified earlier you noted the blood on the sofa where the victim was lying?

A: Yes, sir.

Q: Notice anything else on the sofa?

A: What do you mean, sir?

Q: Did you find a bullet there behind his back?

A: I didn't see any bullet, sir.

Q: You looked for the bullet?

A: I looked sir, yes sir, but there was a lot of blood there. When I didn't see any I figured it must still be in his back.

Q: So your answer is you found no bullet on the sofa?

A: That is correct, sir.

Q: See any bullet hole?

A: You mean in the sofa, sir?

Q: That's exactly what I mean. If a bullet came out his back it would have left some kind of hole in the sofa, wouldn't it?

"Objection!"

"Sustained!"

Q: I will ask you again. Did you see any bullet hole in the sofa?

A: Sir, as I said, the sofa was covered with blood—

Q: So, you didn't see any bullet hole?

A: No, sir.

"Thank you, Officer. Your Honor, I wish to recall Dr. Vasconcelos as my final witness."

As the doctor resumes the stand, Bourne goes to the large diagram the doctor drew earlier.

Q: Doctor, you drew this diagram showing the angle of the bullet that entered the chest?

A: Yes, sir.

You can tell the doctor is wondering what the attorney is getting at.

Q: You said you placed the victim in this horizontal position because you assumed that was his position when shot?

A: Yes.

Q: The bullet did come out his back, did it not?

A: It had to, yes.

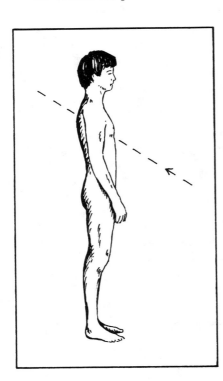

Q: And knowing the path of the bullet, would it be your opinion that if he were lying down on the sofa in this horizontal position, faceup, the bullet would have one into the sofa upon exiting his back?

"Objection!"

"Overruled. You may answer, Doctor."

A: I would say so, yes.

Bourne then turns the diagram on its side.

Q: Suppose, Doctor, we look at your diagram this way.

(See diagram at left.)

Q: In this position, with the victim in a standing position, the shooter down below: is this also consistent with your finding as to the angle of entry?

A: It is.

"That's all. Thank you, Doctor, you've been very helpful."

Possible verdicts:
1. Guilty of first degree murder
2. Guilty of second degree murder
3. Guilty of voluntary manslaughter
4. Not guilty

WHAT IS YOUR VERDICT?

[Before choosing your verdict, see Jury Instructions 1–3, 5–13, 15, starting on page 197.]

QUESTIONS AND ANALYSIS

Q1. The pathologist's diagram showed the victim lying in a horizontal position when shot. How did the defense attorney put this diagram to the defendant's advantage?

Q2. In order to prove first degree murder, the prosecution must show the killing is willful, deliberate, and premeditated with malice aforethought. What two pieces of evidence in particular could be used by the prosecutor to attribute these qualities to Maria Carvalho prior to the shooting?

Q3. How did the defense attorney damage the credibility of two key witnesses for the prosecution?

Q4. What evidence of noise or lack of noise prior to the shooting was helpful to the prosecution in rebutting the defense claim of self-defense?

Q5. What glaring error of investigation was made by the police officer who searched the apartment?

Q6. Suppose you found that Maria Carvalho was not in immediate danger when she killed her husband but shot him out of a reasonable fear that he would harm her seriously in the near future. Does that justify her action in your mind? Could her attorney use the "battered woman's syndrome" evidence to help her?

Q7. Suppose you found that Maria Carvalho was not in immediate danger but fired in an honest but unreasonable fear that she was. What would your verdict be? In this situation would the battered woman's syndrome evidence have greater relevance?

A1. The defense attorney in this case made several smart moves. One of the best had to do with his handling of the pathologist's diagram showing the victim lying in a horizontal position when shot, the bullet entering his body from above.

Bourne simply turned the diagram on its side, which then showed the victim in a vertical or standing position, the bullet now appearing to enter from below. This position would lend credibility to the defense argument that Maria got the gun out to commit suicide after the fight the previous evening, as she testified, and when her husband advanced toward her in her bed to beat her again, she fired to defend herself. And there was the state's own diagram to show exactly how it happened.

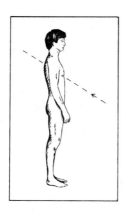 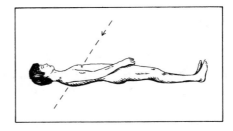

A2. Two pieces of evidence, in particular, could be used to support the element of deliberation and premeditation: 1) the testimony of the neighbor Caetano that Maria told him several days before the incident she was thinking of killing her husband if the violence continued, and 2) the fact that she waited six seconds—ample time to weigh her decision—before firing the third shot.

A3. The defense attorney, in his cross-examination, managed to cast doubt on the credibility first of the victim's close friend, Castro. The fact that he had been convicted of two felonies, one of which involved dishonesty, could be considered by the jury in deciding if they could believe him. The second was the female prisoner, Salazar. By getting her to admit she hoped to gain favor with the prosecution by her testimony, the defense counsel impeached her credibility. Her notes of the alleged conversation with the defendant were never found in the jail locker, which also damaged her status as a witness.

A4. There were no sounds heard by the neighbors just before the shots to indicate any struggle or beating; no screaming or crying of a woman in fear. The lack of such evidence supports the prosecutor's argument that Maria fired, not in self-defense, but in cold blood.

A5. Three shots were fired. One bullet was found in the wall. Another was still lodged in the victim's shoulder. Where was the third bullet? Apparently the police never found it. The officer who searched the apartment made a glaring mistake in failing to search for the third bullet or a bullet hole in the sofa where the body was found. It was obvious from cross-examination he neglected to make a careful probe because of so much blood in that spot. The fact that there was blood on the sofa behind the victim's back doesn't mean he was shot there. He could have been shot while standing, then fallen back on the sofa. Evidence of either the bullet or bullet hole would have been the strongest possible circumstantial evidence that the victim was shot while lying down on the sofa.

A6. Under existing U.S. law, the right of self-defense is available to the killer only when the danger to one's life is immediate, not at some future time. Therefore if Maria fired because she feared her husband would harm her in the near future, the right of self-defense is not available to her. The law says that no matter how severely her husband may have injured her in the past, her use of deadly force is not justified unless it appeared necessary to protect her from immediate death or great bodily injury. Evidence of the "battered woman's syndrome" will not help her in this situation.

There is considerable criticism of this law of self-defense, and some lawyers argue that it is too rigid, that deadly force should be justified even when the danger isn't so immediate—when the woman feels so trapped by an abusive relationship that she sees no other way out. There seems to be growing support for a change in the law, which would give a battered woman in certain abusive relationships the right of self-defense when she kills to avoid an inevitable fatal result, when she kills not in retaliation for an immediate threat but to prevent abuse that she reasonably believes will reoccur.

A7. As part of the change occurring throughout the United States in this area of law, some states now allow evidence of the "battered woman's syndrome" to help the defendant who is not in immediate danger but has an honest belief that she is so because of past abuse. If the jury finds the woman defendant had an honest but unreasonable belief that she was in immediate danger, the jury is instructed that the verdict should be voluntary manslaughter rather than murder. Such a finding does not, however, warrant acquittal.

VERDICT

GUILTY OF MURDER IN THE FIRST DEGREE

After a long night of deliberation, the jury found Maria Carvalho guilty of first degree murder.

The defense attorney's use of the state's diagram was a simple but brilliant stroke, except—as so often happens with brilliant strokes in jury trials—the jury did not accept it.

(Sentence: Twenty-seven Years to Life in Prison)

STATE *v.* BUCKLES

You are juror number ten in a case charging the attempted rape of a white woman by a black man, and you have been selected after long and vigorous questioning by the defense attorney.

"Do you have any feelings about black people that would prevent you from being fair?" "Do you think blacks as a group tend to commit more crimes of violence than whites?" "Would you find this charge less offensive if the defendant were white?" "Have any black friends?" "What would you say if you were in a social group and someone made a racial slur against blacks?"

Finally sworn in and seated in the jury box, you look again at the defendant, Gary Buckles. He is a young African-American, slim and handsome, well dressed in a conservative business suit. His attorney, Marina Phelps, is also black. Judging by her appearance, she must be just out of law school and she sits quietly, almost meekly at her counsel table, waiting for the district attorney to call his first witness.

The burly D.A., Michael Lyons, looks very sure of himself. He has been strutting across the room like a drum major, a man in charge. In a booming voice, he calls Lorraine Eberhart to the stand.

You hear a gasp in the courtroom as she comes in. She is a striking beauty with long blond hair. You watch her take her place slowly, like a queen, on the witness stand. Lorraine Eberhart . . . You remember the D.A. gave her name as the victim of the attempted rape. You look at her. You look at the defendant. Are you really unbiased after all? Your reaction catches you by surprise. And now you understand why his attorney had to ask all those questions.

Miss Eberhart testifies she is twenty years old and lives with her room-mate, Priscilla Mackey, in a two-bedroom apartment on the second floor of a large complex. She says she works as a restaurant hostess and that on the evening in question she came home around midnight. Feeling tired, she went to bed about 1:00 A.M. but was awakened an hour later by Priscilla and her boyfriend, Troy. They insisted she get up and join them for some Chinese food and beer they had just brought home. She put on her robe, went into the living room, and shared the food and beer with Priscilla and Troy.

At about 4:00 A.M. Miss Eberhart claims she went back to bed. Her bed-room is on one side of the living room, Miss Mackey's bedroom on the other. The living room has a sliding glass door opening onto the balcony, which overlooks a large patio below, and her bedroom window looks out on the balcony. When she went to bed she locked the window and the front door but did not lock the sliding glass door, since Priscilla and Troy were still up and she thought they would take care of that.

Lorraine was wearing a T-shirt and underpants when she got in bed; she fell asleep immediately. She was awakened suddenly to find a man kneeling beside her in her bed, his face above her. He was wearing a white turtleneck sweater, which he pulled up over his head as soon as she awoke. He had his head down, and he was grabbing at her underpants, trying to pull them off. She pushed him away, fighting him. For some rea-son, she does not know why, she didn't scream right away. The man tried to kiss her with the sweater pulled up partly covering his face. A violent struggle ensued while he kept tugging at her underpants. She was pushing him and kicking him. She kept telling him to go away. When he tried to lie on top of her, she screamed.

He ran out immediately. She could hear him climbing over the balcony. Priscilla and Troy, asleep in Priscilla's room, rushed in and she told them what had happened. They ran out to the living room and noticed the slid-ing glass door open. They looked over the balcony but saw nothing in the dim light. Troy called the police, and fifteen minutes later they came. The police asked Lorraine to describe her attacker, but all she could say was that he was a young black man wearing a white sweater.

Now D.A. Lyons moves to a different line of questioning.

Q: Had you ever seen this man before?

A: Not to my knowledge.

Q: Did you authorize him to enter your apartment?

A: Of course not.

Q: Did he touch any part of your body with his hands?

A: Yes. He touched my breast . . . my left breast.

Q: Did you authorize him to touch your left breast?

A: Absolutely not.

Q: Were you afraid?

A: Yes. Of course.

Q: Did he ever get your underpants off?

A: No.

Q: Did he ever kiss you?

A: No.

Q: I want you to look around this courtroom. Do you see the man who tried to rape you?

"Yes." She points to the defendant. "That's him."

Q: You're positive?

A: Yes.

Obviously pleased with the answers, Lyons smiles at Miss Phelps as if to say, "See if you can get around that."

Miss Phelps keeps her seat, checking her notes. She is a soft-spoken young woman and seems a bit intimidated by the task, but she is determined as she asks her questions.

Q: You were very tired that morning before you went back to bed?

A: Yes.

Q: How much beer did you have before you went back to bed?

A: A couple cans.

Q: How many?

A: Two or three. I didn't count.

Q: Could have been four?

"Objection!" the D.A. says. "The witness says she doesn't know."

"Sustained."

Q: Did you take anything else?

A: I ate some Chinese food.

Q: Anything else?

A: What do you mean?

Q: Did you take anything else—any other chemicals—into your system?

A: Well, yes, we smoked.

Q: Smoked what?

A: Well . . . yeah . . . they had some pot.

Q: Marijuana?

A: Yes.

Q: Who did?

A: Me and Troy. He gave me some.

Q: How did you smoke it?

A: Through a pipe—it's called a bong.

Q: Tell the jury how it works.

A: Well, it's a long vertical pipe, a water pipe. You put the marijuana in the bowl of the bong, then you light it up and inhale it.

Miss Phelps nods as if she is very interested in how it works.

Q: And how much did you have?

A: One or two hits.

Q: A hit? What's a hit? Tell the jury what a hit is.

A: Each bowl is called a hit.

Q: And you had some hits along with the beer?

A: Yes.

Q: Did you have lipstick on that night?

A: Yes.

Q: Rouge?

A: Just a little.

Q: Did you wash your makeup off before you went to bed?

A: No, but it doesn't stay on that long.

Under further cross-examination, Miss Eberhart testifies the bedroom was quite dark, the curtains drawn. She says that during the struggle she may have scratched her attacker with her fingernails.

Q: How long was he in the room?

A: I didn't look at my watch. It seemed like a long time. Maybe twenty minutes.

Q: What happened for twenty minutes?

A: I was fighting him off.

Q: Miss Eberhart, isn't it true you saw him only through the opening in the sweater?

A: No, I saw his whole face when I woke up. Then he pulled his sweater up.

Miss Phelps walks up to the witness with a report. "I show you this police report. I ask you to read it to yourself to see if it refreshes your memory."

The witness reads it over and then says, "I read it."

Q: Does it refresh your memory that you told the officer you saw the man only through the opening in the sweater?

A: I might have said that. I was very upset. But I'm sure it's him.

Now the D.A. calls Lorraine's roommate, Priscilla Mackey. She too is young and pretty, also with long blond hair. She corroborates Lorraine's account of how the two women and her boyfriend, Troy, had Chinese food and beer that night. She admits that Lorraine smoked marijuana, but does not think it affected her. In Priscilla's opinion, Lorraine was not intoxicated, just tired. Priscilla says she didn't smoke marijuana because she doesn't believe in it. She and Troy were asleep when she heard Lorraine's screams. They rushed into Lorraine's bedroom and found her crying and hysterical. They ran to the balcony to see if they could see anyone, but the man was gone. She says she feels guilty because she had forgotten to lock the sliding glass door.

The D.A. marches over to the defendant, stands directly behind him, and points dramatically at Buckles.

Q: You ever see this man before that night?

A: Yes.

Q: Where did you see him?

A: He'd just moved into our apartment complex. His apartment is just across the patio from ours, on the ground floor. Lorraine's never seen him, but I have.

Q: How's that?

A: A few nights before this happened, Lorraine and I were walking from the pool back to our place. We were in our bathing suits. I saw him standing at his window.

Q: What did you notice?

A: Lorraine was walking ahead of me, because she was in a hurry. I noticed him looking at her. He kept watching her as she walked by. She didn't notice him, but I did.

Q: You are sure this is the same man you saw staring at her?

A: I'm positive.

Again, the defense attorney remains seated as she conducts cross.

Q: Miss Mackey, isn't it a fact you suspected my client was the one who tried to rape her right from the start?

A: Sure. Soon as she told me it was a black guy.

Q: And when the police came you told them right away you were sure he was the one?

A: Yes. He lived right there. The way he looked at her and all. He fit the description.

Q: The description being of a young black man?

A: Yes.

Officer Joe Sampino testifies he was the first officer on the scene. He says his partner, Officer Gonzales, stayed on the ground checking out the complex for possible suspects while Sampino went upstairs to Lorraine's apartment. He took the account from her as best he could although she was still crying from fright.

He inspected the apartment for point of entry and concluded the attacker must have noticed the open sliding door, climbed up the red brick pillar to the balcony, and entered through the sliding door. He must have exited the same way. When Priscilla told him she believed it was the new neighbor across the patio, he directed Officer Gonzales over the walkie-talkie to go to the defendant's front door and ask him to come outside to a point where he and Lorraine could see him from her window. Officer Sampino explains that he wanted to see if Lorraine could make a positive identification. He and Lorraine stood at the window and watched Officer Gonzales ring the doorbell, then bang on the door, and wait for the defendant. After a long wait they saw the door open, Gonzales gesture, and the defendant, dressed in a bathrobe, step outside. As soon as he did Lorraine gasped and said, "That's him!" Sampino immediately directed Gonzales over the radio to place the defendant under arrest.

Lyons is beaming. "Your witness, Counsel," he says to Miss Phelps, who checks her notes carefully before she begins.

Q: Officer, did Miss Eberhart tell you that she saw the man only through the opening in the sweater?

A: May I check my notes?

Q: Please.

A: [after checking his report] Yes, she did.

Q: Did she have any doubt about her ability to identify him?

A: At first she did.

Q: What do you mean?

A: When I told her what we were going to do, that I was going to have him step outside his door to see if she could identify him, she hesitated. She said she didn't think she could. But as soon as she saw him there was no problem.

Q: How far away was he?

A: Oh, about seventy feet.

Q: Was it light yet?

A: It was dawn, just getting light.

Q: And he was standing right beside the officer in uniform?

A: Yes.

Miss Phelps pauses. She stands up for the first time and takes a deep breath. She is more aggressive now and seems more sure of herself.

Q: You know what a lineup is, Officer?

A: Of course.

Q: You've conducted lineups, haven't you?

A: Yes. Numerous times.

Q: Officer Sampino, please tell the jury what a lineup is.

"Objection! Irrelevant."

"Overruled. You may answer."

A: A lineup is where we have the suspect stand in line with five or six others of similar appearance, and the witness is asked to look them over carefully and see if he or she can pick out the one who did it.

Q: And that is done to make sure you have a positive identification, right, Officer?

A: Yes.

Q: And it's done to make sure there is no improper suggestion made by the police to the witness that might influence her?

A: That's true.

Q: It's done in the interest of fairness, right, Officer? You wouldn't want to arrest an innocent man?

A: That's right.

Miss Phelps sits down again. There is a long pause.

Q: This wasn't a lineup, was it, Officer?

The officer looks at the D.A.

"No," he says, "I guess not."

The last witness for the prosecution is the arresting officer, Ramon Gonzales. He testifies that after placing the defendant under arrest he received instructions over the radio from Officer Sampino to search the defendant's apartment for a white turtleneck sweater. Gonzales says he advised Buckles of his rights, then asked him if he had a white turtleneck sweater. Buckles said he did and led the officer back to his closet where he dug out a sweater, which Gonzales immediately confiscated for evidence. It was white and had a turtleneck. Gonzales took it outside, looked up at the window where Lorraine and Officer Sampino were still watching. He held the sweater up so they could see it, and Lorraine made a circle with her thumb and forefinger as if to say, "That's it."

The D.A. draws out a white sweater from a bag on his table, has it marked by the clerk, and shows it to Officer Gonzales. The officer identifies it as the one he took.

Later, at Sampino's request, Gonzales says he went up to the crime scene to dust for fingerprints. He found none of evidentiary value. The identifiable prints belonged to Lorraine, Priscilla, Troy, and one of Lorraine's boyfriends. The others were too smudged for identification.

Miss Phelps now takes over.

Q: Did you inspect the sweater?

A: Visually, yes.

Q: Was it wet, as if it had just been washed?

A: No.

Q: See any stains on it, like lipstick or rouge?

A: I didn't see any.

Q: Any blond hairs on it?

A: No.

Miss Phelps picks up the sweater, which is still lying on the witness stand in front of the officer.

Q: You placed this sweater in the police evidence locker?

A: Yes.

Q: No one else touched it?

A: No.

Miss Phelps turns to the judge. "Your Honor, I ask that this sweater be passed among the jurors so they may see it close up."

"Motion granted," the judge says.

She hands the sweater to juror number one, who looks it over and passes it on. When it comes to you, you study it carefully. You don't see any marks on it, no hairs or stains. It is spotless.

"You may proceed," the judge says to Miss Phelps after each juror examines the sweater.

"What about Mr. Buckles," the defense attorney says. "See any scratches on him?"

"I didn't see any," the officer replies.

Q: Did you look him over carefully?

A: Yes.

Miss Phelps looks satisfied.

The prosecution, having no further witnesses, rests its case.

Gary Buckles takes the stand in his defense. He answers the questions in a quiet, straightforward manner. He says he is a sophomore at State College and has a part-time job as a waiter. About two weeks before the incident he moved into the apartment on the ground floor with another student, Max Friedrich. They each have their own bedroom. That evening Buckles says he came home from work about 10:00 P.M., decided to go to a late movie by himself, and went out again. He came home about 1:00 A.M., read for a while, went to bed, and did not leave his room until he was awakened in the morning by the police banging on his door.

He acknowledges that he owns a white turtleneck sweater, which he keeps in his closet, but says he hadn't worn it in a while and gave it to the officer upon request. He doesn't know Lorraine Eberhart but admits he saw her once when she walked by his apartment in her bathing suit, and he thought she was very attractive. He denies entering her apartment that morning and trying to rape her. He says he's willing to submit to a lie detector test.

Miss Phelps asks him to face the jury, look the jurors in the eye, and tell them if he did it. He turns and faces you directly.

"I didn't do it," he says quietly. "I swear it. I didn't try to rape that girl. No way. You got to believe me."

The D.A. begins his cross. He has a faint smirk on his face, as if he doesn't believe anything Buckles says.

Q: What went through your mind the first time you saw Lorraine Eberhart?

A: I don't understand.

Q: You understand all right, Mr. Buckles. A few days before this incident, you watched her walk by in her bathing suit. What were you thinking then?

A: I thought she was very nice.

Q: She looked good to you?

A: Well, yes.

Q: You looked at her?

A: Yes. I don't deny that.

Q: You found her attractive?

A: She's attractive, yes.

Q: You felt an attraction for her?

A: I wouldn't say that.

Q: Isn't it a fact you went back inside and made a comment about her to your roommate, Max?

A: I may have.

Q: Didn't you make a comment to him about the size of her breasts?

A: I don't remember what I said.

Q: Didn't you say to him, "Man, you should have seen the size of the boobs that just went by." Didn't you say that?

A: I may have.

Q: And didn't you make a gesture with your hands describing her breasts? Didn't you do that also?

A: That's possible.

Q: And didn't you, thereafter, form the specific intent in your mind to make sexual contact with her?

A: Look, I thought she had a real nice figure. But that's it. I didn't break into her place that night, and I didn't try to rape her.

Max Friedrich, Buckles's roommate, now testifies he has been Buckles's friend for four years. They met in high school, went to the same college, then agreed to move in together in the new apartment off campus. They have separate bedrooms, one adjoining bathroom. Friedrich says he arrived home that night at about eleven o'clock, after the library closed. Buckles was not home, and Friedrich went to bed and didn't wake up until early the next morning, when he heard the police at the door.

He says he'd seen Buckles earlier that evening, and he was not wearing his white sweater. He didn't hear his roommate come in or go out. He remembers Buckles commenting to him about Lorraine Eberhart's breast size, but they often made such comments to each other about girls who walked by in bathing suits, and he thought nothing of Buckles's remark. He is well acquainted with Buckles's reputation for character traits of nonviolence and honesty, and his reputation is good. He has never known Buckles to be a violent person.

Next Miss Phelps calls Mary McElhaney, a criminologist for the police department. She states that she was trained at the University of California at Berkeley in the science of detecting various types of stains on cloth. She examined the sweater removed from the defendant's residence under the microscope and found no evidence of lipstick or rouge. She found several strands of hair on the sweater and compared them with several hairs removed from the head of Lorraine Eberhart, but they did not match.

Miss Phelps is poker-faced as she continues her questioning.

Q: At my request did you also examine the red brick pillars supporting the balcony of the victim's residence?

A: I did.

Q: And did you find any similar substance on the sweater?

A: I did not.

Q: In your opinion would particles of the red brick pillar be likely to adhere to such a sweater worn by a person climbing up or down those pillars?

D.A.: Objection! Speculation!

Judge: Sustained. You may not answer.

As her last witness, Miss Phelps recalls Lorraine Eberhart, who has been sitting in the audience. The D.A. looks surprised.

A: Ma'am, you remember when the officer, Officer Sampino, asked you if you thought you could identify the man who tried to rape you?

A: Yes, we were by the window.

Q: Do you remember what you said?

A: No, I don't remember what I said. I was so upset.

Q: I appreciate that, ma'am. But Officer Sampino has testified in this courtroom that you said you didn't think you could identify the man. Is that true?

A: If he testified to it, I must have said it. But what's the difference? I was able to identify him when I saw him.

Q: Yes, I realize that, ma'am, but could you tell us why you didn't think you could identify him?

A: Well . . . because . . .

She is looking at the D.A.

Q: Please look at me, Miss Eberhart. Please tell me and tell this jury. Why didn't you think you could identify the man who attacked you?

A: Well . . . because . . .

Q: Because why?

A: Well . . . because . . . all blacks look alike to me.

Miss Phelps stares at the witness. There is dead silence. The D.A. is grimly shaking his head.

———

Possible verdicts:
1. Guilty of attempted rape
2. Not guilty

WHAT IS YOUR VERDICT?

[Before choosing your verdict, see Jury Instructions 1–3, 5, 18, starting on page 197.]

QUESTIONS AND ANALYSIS

Q1.   What was the single most damaging testimony to the prosecution's case?

Q2.   Did the police use a fair identification procedure when they asked the victim to see if she could identify the suspect at a distance of seventy feet while he stood beside a uniformed police officer?

Q3.   Why didn't the police wait to conduct a lineup at the station before they arrested the defendant?

Q4.   What was the significance of the absence of any lipstick, rouge, and hair, or particles from the red brick pillars, on the sweater belonging to the defendant?

Q5.   In the cross-examination of Lorraine Eberhart as to her ingestion of marijuana and beer, did the defense attorney miss a good opportunity to raise a doubt as to Lorraine's identification?

Q6.   Since the defense attorney had the criminologist available as an expert witness, should she have also used the criminologist to testify as to the effect of marijuana and beer?

Q7.   Was the intruder a professional burglar?

———

A1.   The statement of six words by the victim, Lorraine Eberhart—"All blacks look alike to me"—was the single most damaging piece of evidence to the prosecution's case. In a close case of identification, that statement was devastating.

A2. The identification procedure was not entirely fair. Legal opinions agree that showing a suspect singly beside a police officer for the victim to identify has an element of suggestiveness. Despite its potential unfairness, the courts will generally balance the interests involved and allow the evidence of such an identification to be presented to the jury and let the jurors decide for themselves whether it is reliable. However, if the identification is shown to be so unfair as to deprive the defendant of due process of law, the judge will suppress it altogether. To some jurors Eberhart's cross-racial identification of a black man under these circumstances would raise a serious question as to its reliability.

A3. There is no question that a lineup at the police station, where Buckles would stand in a line of five or six men whose appearance is similar to his, would be a fairer identification procedure for him rather than the single-person "show-up." But generally the law does not require the police to wait for a lineup. That is because any possible unfairness is considered offset by the likelihood that a prompt identification within a short time after the crime will be more accurate than a belated identification days or weeks later. Furthermore the police say, and the courts agree, that it is as important to free an innocent person promptly from suspicion as it is to identify a guilty person.

A4. Since the victim did not wash her makeup off before going to bed, she probably still had some lipstick and rouge on her face at the time of the attack. She had long blond hair, which might have brushed against the sweater in the struggle. The most likely point of entry and exit was by way of the red brick pillars leading to the balcony, which the intruder would have had to rub against in climbing up and down. The lack of any such marks on the sweater was a strong point in the defense case.

A5. Yes, Lorraine's admission that she smoked marijuana and drank beer just before retiring left her vulnerable to attack on cross-examination. The reason one inhales marijuana through a bong like the one she used is to obtain a stronger effect than from a marijuana cigarette. Mixing marijuana and beer together affects one's powers of observation. Miss Phelps, lacking in experience, missed an opportunity to cast doubt on Lorraine's identification when she failed to emphasize this point.

A6.   Yes, Phelps should have used the criminologist to testify as to scientific studies that show the effect on the mind caused by mixing marijuana and alcohol.

A7.   No. The man who broke into the apartment and attacked Lorraine Eberhart wore a white sweater. No professional burglar or sophisticated criminal would dress like that. They always wear dark clothing, which aids concealment and is less likely to pick up telltale evidence.

VERDICT

NOT GUILTY

For purposes of this book, the Buckles case combines facts of two actual trials. Had the jurors heard the case as presented here, we believe they would have acquitted Buckles because of the questionable evidence as to identification.

STATE v. BARKER

You are juror number eleven in the case of Henry Barker, charged with the murder of his wife, Edith, for $30,000 of insurance money.

The situation sounds banal, but the judge makes it less so when he says there will be evidence that someone else may have been involved in the crime.

"You must not give any consideration," he says, "as to why the other person or persons are not being prosecuted in this trial or whether they have been or will be prosecuted."

The D.A., Mary Ward, is noticeably pregnant. But as you will see, that doesn't prevent her from being a forceful prosecuting attorney. As she outlines the evidence you wonder whether this is a real case or a piece of detective fiction. The classic elements are all here—a drug deal, $5,000 in blood money, a key witness with a lapsed memory, a hit man, a mysterious phone call, and a woman boarder suspected of being romantically involved with the defendant, Barker.

The defense attorney, Sarah Frizelle, portly and formidable-looking, rises, and in a cold, clipped voice she derides the state's case with incisive sarcasm.

"You've heard a lot of words like a laundry list from the district attorney. A $5,000 payoff? We will show such money was never paid or never even existed. Those so-called mysterious words on the phone: see for yourself if they have any meaning in this case." At this point she moves behind the defendant and places both hands protectively on his shoulders. He is tall, lean, well dressed in a gray suit. "Just remember," she says, "this man, Henry Barker, is presumed innocent. He *doesn't have to prove anything. The only burden is on the prosecution to prove him guilty beyond any reasonable doubt. That's the law.*

"You took an oath to follow that law. I know you will do so."

Mary Ward calls the first witness for the prosecution. He is Milton Ordway, Henry Barker's friend and next-door neighbor. About a week before the murder, Henry came over to Ordway's house.

Q: What did he want?

A: He wanted to talk about his insurance policies. I was selling insurance then, and he wanted some advice.

Q: Did you give him advice?

A: Yes, I did. After looking over his policies I told him he had too much life insurance on his wife and not enough on himself, since he was the breadwinner. So I advised him to reverse the amounts.

Q: Did he agree to do that?

A: Yes. I drew up an application for new policies and set up an appointment for him to take a physical. The company wouldn't approve the policy without the physical.

Q: Did he take the physical?

A: No. He missed the appointment.

Q: So the old policies were still in effect at the time of Mrs. Barker's death?

A: Yes.

Q: For how much?

A: About $30,000 on her, $10,000 on him.

Q: And to your knowledge was that amount paid to him by the company after her death?

A: Yes, it was.

Ordway testifies that on the evening of Edith Barker's death, he and his wife had a crystal party for the purpose of selling crystalware to their friends. Henry was teaching at the navy school that night. Edith was present but seemed unusually quiet and fidgety. He gave her the doctor's card to give to Henry for the physical. She fingered it nervously and looked it over, but he noticed that when she left at about nine-thirty, the card was still on the table.

Sometime after 10:30 P.M. he was awakened by the constant ringing of the doorbell. When he answered it, Sally Lester was at the door.

Q: Who's Sally Lester?

A: She's a female boarder who rents a room at the Barkers' house. She and Henry are both in the navy—he's an instructor, she's a student—and sometimes they ride to navy night school together and come home together.

Q: Ever notice any romantic involvement between them?

A: Well . . .

Q: Did you?

A: Well, you know . . . the neighbors talk, but I never noticed anything.

"Objection, Your Honor, as to what neighbors say. That's hearsay."

"Sustained. Jury is admonished to disregard that part of the answer."

Q: What did she want?

A: She said Edith was hurt, and Henry wanted me to come over right away.

Ordway says he got dressed and went next door, where Henry met him outside. They went in together and he saw Edith lying on the floor. She had a cord from the iron around her neck; the iron was on the floor beside her head. She looked dead, so he didn't go up to her. He asked Henry if he had called the police, and Henry said he had. Then the phone rang and Henry answered it.

Q: Could you hear the conversation?

A: It was very brief. He just said: "No, they have not got here yet and, you know, I just can't talk right now!"

Q: Do you know who he was talking to?

A: No. A few seconds later the police came and they took over.

The questioning shifts to a time several months after the murder. Ordway testifies he got out of the insurance business and organized his own company, manufacturing nameplates. Barker loaned him $15,000 to help the company get started, but the business failed and closed down within the year.

Q: Do you know where Barker got the $15,000?

A: He said it came from the insurance proceeds.

Q: Did you ever pay him the money back?

A: No, the money was gone.

Q: Did he ever ask you for it?

A: Not really. He knew we'd lost it.

Q: So the $15,000 has still never been repaid—up to this day?

A: That's right.

Defense Attorney Sarah Frizelle starts her cross-examination with a frontal attack.

Q: Mr. Ordway, you studied first aid in the Marine Corps, didn't you?

A: Yes.

Q: In fact you taught first aid to the marines for several years, is that true?

A: Yes.

Q: So you were an expert in first aid?

A: You might say that.

Q: When you saw Edith Barker lying on the floor, did you go over to check her?

A: No.

Q: Did you check to see if she was alive? her vital signs?

A: No.

Q: Why didn't you do that, Mr. Ordway?

A: Well, I was in shock, that's why. And besides, Henry told me she was dead.

Q: Do you know if Henry checked her?

A: I don't know.

Q: When you saw Henry outside the house was he upset?

A: Yes, he was.

Q: Was he crying?

A: Yes.

Q: He was reacting as any husband would normally react upon finding his wife murdered?

"Objection, Your Honor. As to how a husband normally reacts."

"Overruled. You may answer."

A: Yes. He was shocked.

Q: What about Sally Lester?

A: What about her?

Q: Didn't you tell police you were surprised by her reactions?

A: Yes.

Q: What did you mean?

A: Well, when she first came to the door she seemed very quiet, sub-dued—not excited at all.

Q: Did she ever come back to ask what happened to Mrs. Barker?

A: No.

Q: Did she ever ask anyone to your knowledge if Edith Barker was alive or dead?

A: No.

Q: Did she at any time that evening express any interest in the condition of Edith Barker?

A: No, that's what surprised me.

Sally Lester takes the stand for the prosecution. She is an attractive brunette in her early thirties, athletic-looking. She wears a sweater and skirt. She doesn't look at Barker, seated at counsel table. In fact, she keeps herself turned away from him as she speaks. Under questioning by prosecutor Mary Ward, she testifies that she met Henry Barker when they were both in the navy eight years ago. She was a student at the navy electronics school; he was an instructor. They were not in the same class, but there were several classes close together, and during breaks students and instructors would get together in the lounge. Sally and Henry struck up a friendship. About two months before the murder, Sally asked Barker if he knew of a room she could rent. He invited her to rent the extra room in his house, so she did. Edith did not object.

Q: Who lived in the residence when you moved in?

A: Henry and Edith Barker.

Q: Were there any children?

A: No.

Q: What was the house like?

A: Two bedrooms, one bath, living room, kitchen-dining room, garage.

Q: You had one of the bedrooms?

A: Yes.

Q: They were next to each other?

A: Yes.

Q: Was there ever any romantic relationship between you and Henry?

A: No.

Q: You're sure?

A: Well, we were affectionate. We were fond of each other. But that was it.

Several weeks before the murder, Sally says she met Leonard Keck. He was also an instructor at the navy school, and they began having drinks together after class. Late one night, while the Barkers were asleep, she brought Keck home to her room, where he slept with her; he left before the Barkers awoke. Keck told her that he, Keck, was a hit man. She understood the term "hit man" to mean someone who kills people for money, but she didn't take him seriously. When she told Barker what Keck said, Barker replied, "Why don't you see if he wants a job?" During one of the breaks at school she introduced the two men to each other and observed them talking. A few days before the murder, Barker gave her a note, folded and stapled, to deliver to Keck, which she did. She has no idea what it said.

On the night of the murder Barker drove her home from school. He opened the door with his keys. As they started inside, Barker stopped her and said, "Go get Milt and tell him to come right over." She went to get Ordway, and then stayed at his house all night while the police investigated the murder scene.

Once again Sarah Frizelle opens her cross by going straight for the jugular.

Q: You didn't like Edith, did you?

A: We got along.

Q: Didn't she accuse you of having an affair with Henry?

A: I don't remember.

Q: Let me refresh your memory, Miss Lester. Do you remember one afternoon when Edith surprised you in your room as she came in to get sheets off the bed—

A: What are you talking about?

Q: —and you were just getting dressed and Mr. Barker was in the shower: do you remember that?

A: Something like that, yes.

Q: And do you remember what she said when she saw damp stains on the bottom sheet?

A: Yes. She made an accusation, but there was nothing to it.

Q: That made you mad, didn't it?

A: That's true.

Q: You wanted to get rid of her, didn't you?

A: Don't be silly.

Q: You wanted to live in the house alone with Mr. Barker, didn't you?

A: No. That's nonsense.

Q: Nonsense? Isn't that what you did? Didn't you go on living in the house with Mr. Barker after Edith's death?

A: Well, yes . . .

Q: Tell the jury how long you continued to live in the house with Mr. Barker after Edith's death.

A: Three months.

Q: Did you sleep in the master bedroom?

"Objection!"

"Sustained!"

Frizelle turns sharply to the judge. She looks upset. "But, Your Honor . . ." She cannot let the ruling pass. "My question goes to her motive—her motive to get Edith Barker out of the way, her motive to lie about that. If she slept with—"

"It's irrelevant," Ward shouts. "Irrelevant and ridiculous!"

The judge leans back, stroking his chin. He looks at the two women attorneys, both standing, waiting anxiously.

"I'll reverse my ruling," the judge says. He leans over to Sally Lester. "You may answer the question."

"What was the question?" Lester asks. "I've forgotten the question."

"I'll gladly state it again," Frizelle replies.

Q: Did you sleep in the master bedroom?

A: No, I did not. He slept in his room. I slept in mine.

The D.A. calls Jack Wister next. He comes through the door with a swagger, shabbily dressed, unshaven, his shirt hanging partly out of his pants. He looks like a man who has had a hard night, or more accurately, several hard nights. Wister testifies he used to be best friends with the Barkers. He and his wife, Jeannette, socialized with them often before Edith's death. He tells of a conversation he had with Barker about a month before the murder. They'd both been drinking. Henry was upset with Edith because she'd had an extramarital affair while he was on a navy cruise in the Mediterranean.

Q: Did he ask you to kill Edith?

A: Not directly, but he asked if it could be done.

Q: What did you say?

A: I said it was possible, but I didn't want to have anything to do with it.

Q: Did he ask how much it would cost?

A: Yes, and I told him five thousand dollars.

Q: Did he say where the money would come from?

A: Yes, he said it would come from the insurance.

Q: What did he say when you said you wouldn't do it?

A: He said if I wouldn't do it, he'd find someone who would.

It is Frizelle's turn to question.

Q: Are you still friends with Henry Barker?

A: D'ya think I'd be sitting here testifying against him if I was?

Q: In fact, you didn't tell this story to the police until you had a falling out with him years after the murder, is that right?

A: True.

Q: Why didn't you tell police about it seven years ago, when they first questioned you?

A: Because I didn't like the detective in charge.

Q: Is that because he had arrested you so many times?

A: Yeah, he was always hassling me.

Q: And some of the arrests resulted in convictions, didn't they?

A: Some did.

Q: Such as burglary and possession of heroin?

A: Yeah, I guess.

Q: And didn't he suspect you of being involved in this murder?

A: Yes.

Q: In fact, he told you he had an eyewitness who saw two people running from the house at the time of the murder, and the description matched you and your wife: isn't that right?

"Objection, Your Honor," Mary Ward says. "It's hearsay as to what the detective said."

"Your Honor," Sarah Frizelle says, "this is an exception to the hearsay rule. It goes to show why he is trying to shift the blame from himself to the defendant. It's not being offered for the truth of the matter."

Judge: For that limited purpose, I will allow it. Objection overruled. You may answer, Mr. Wister.

A: Yeah, that's what the detective said. But that's bull. We were both home that night.

Q: You say you'd been drinking at the time Barker said this to you?

A: We both were.

Q: Were you on drugs?

A: Naah . . .

Q: Marijuana?

A: Oh, yeah, I'd smoked some pot, but I don't consider that a drug.

Q: And you've had a few drinks before you came on the stand today?

A: Well, yeah, a couple. I was nervous.

After Wister, several prosecution witnesses go on and off the stand quickly. The autopsy surgeon confirms Edith was strangled to death, apparently with the cord of her electric iron; the detective testifies there was no evidence of forced entry, that whoever entered apparently came through the back door with a key; the back door was ajar, with the sliding deadbolt protruding. The divorced wife of Leonard Keck testifies that about three months after the murder she saw her husband open an envelope with a large amount of cash in it, but he wouldn't tell her where it came from.

Court adjourns for the day with the announcement by D.A. Mary Ward that her first witness tomorrow will be Amy Gordon. When the trial resumes in the morning you notice the courtroom is filled with spectators waiting to hear her testimony. A TV cameraman is in the back, and the judge asks the jurors if anyone objects to having a TV camera in the court. He promises there will be no shots of the jury. There is no response.

"I have granted the request for television coverage," the judge says, "because I believe the public has a right to know. But if it interferes with a fair trial and the dignity of this court, I will exclude it."

You wonder why this woman Amy Gordon is attracting so much media attention. Then when she enters the courtroom to take the stand you remember having seen her picture in the newspaper recently in connection with this case.

Amy Gordon is a heavyset, timid-looking woman of about thirty-five; she seems stagestruck by all the attention. You notice her taking a deep breath. She testifies she was best friends with Edith Barker before Edith's death. On June 25, 1977, the date Edith was killed, they went shopping together in the afternoon. Edith asked Amy to come over in the evening to keep her company while Henry was teaching. Amy says Edith was feeling depressed because she suspected Henry and Sally were having an affair. Amy promised to come, but when she got home she realized she was tired of hearing Edith's complaints about Henry and decided not to go. Later in the evening she began to feel guilty about not keeping her promise to her best friend. She phoned Edith, but the line was busy. She called again and the line was still busy. Finally she decided to drive over to Edith's herself, although it was past ten. She knocked at the front door but there was no answer. She heard a dull thud and ran around to the back door. The door was ajar with the sliding shaft of the deadbolt lock extended out. She called Edith's name. Still no answer.

Q: What happened then?

A: I turned around and saw a man behind me. He grabbed me around the neck, and I tried to push him off. I fell forward and hit my head. I lunged at him, but he backed away and ran off. I turned back to the door. "Edith!" I shouted. "Edith!" I remember that deadbolt sticking out of the door . . . something about that bolt . . . I looked down and saw her legs, Edith's legs. I heard a cough . . . I went inside. There was Edith lying on the floor. I was in a state of panic. Blood was coming out of her mouth. I couldn't tell if she was breathing or not.

Q: What did you do?

A: Nothing. I walked past her and left through the front door.

Q: Where did you go?

There is a long pause. She is shaking her head.

A: I went home.

Q: Did you try to help her?

A: No, I didn't. Don't ask me why. I don't know why . . .

Q: Did you call the police?

A: No. I went to sleep.

Q: Did you call an ambulance?

A: No.

Q: Why not?

A: I was in shock.

Q: Did you tell your husband?

A: No, no. I didn't tell anyone. Oh, God . . .

There is a murmur through the courtroom.

When she awoke in the morning she'd forgotten it completely. She heard on the radio that Edith had been murdered, and it was as if she was learning the news for the first time. She went to the police on her own that morning to tell them what Edith said, that Henry and Sally were having an affair. The police questioned her at length, but that is all she knew. She had absolutely no recollection of what happened the night before, and this lapse in memory continued for the next six years. During that time, no one was charged with the murder of Edith Barker.

"I'm sorry," Amy Gordon says, shaking her head. "I know it must seem strange to you all."

She testifies that two months ago Detective Dale Phillips reopened the investigation by questioning her again. He had a number of sessions with her, each lasting many hours. Then one night while he was interviewing her for the sixth or seventh time, something strange happened.

Q: Something strange? What was that?

A: He showed me a sketch of the door with the deadbolt sticking out and the feet on the floor. When I saw that deadbolt something just broke inside me. It was like a dam bursting open. It all started to come back. The details of that night came rushing out.

Q: And for the first time your memory of that night came back?

A: Yes.

Q: After six years?

A: Yes.

Q: Do you now remember the man who attacked you by the back door?

A: Yes. He had a scar near his eyes. He was a little taller than me—

Q: Were you able to see his face?

A: Yes, there was a yellow light from the garage.

Q: Do you think you could recognize him if you saw him again?

A: I could try.

The judge nods to the bailiff, and by some prearranged signal the bailiff opens the back door to the courtroom. Another bailiff enters with a prisoner under guard. Amy Gordon looks at the guarded man as if in shock.

View of the back door showing the deadbolt extended. Amy Gordon testified that upon viewing this sketch, the memory of the murder scene came back to her.

"Oh, my God," she shouts, "Oh, my God. It looks like . . . oh, dear . . ." She twists nervously in her seat. Her face is flushed.

"You may proceed," the judge says to the D.A.

Q: Miss Gordon, do you see the man in the courtroom who attacked you that night?

She looks around the room. She studies the prisoner for a long time.

A: Yes . . . He looks like him, it's coming back now, but . . . it's been so long . . . he had a scar near his eyes . . .

She leans forward to see better. "May I go closer?"

Judge: You may.

She steps down and walks up to the prisoner. She peers closely at his face, his eyes, walks around him looking.

A: He looks similar. He has a scar, too . . .

Q: Same height?

A: Yes.

Q: Same build?

A: Yes . . . but . . .

Q: But what?

She shakes her head, returns to the stand.

A: It looks like him, I think it's him, but I can't be sure.

The judge nods to the guard, and he starts to remove the man.

As they reach the door, the judge stops them. "Just a minute," he says, looking at the prisoner. "Would you state your name, sir?"

"Yes, sir," the prisoner says. "My name is Leonard Keck."

"Thank you. You may go."

Gordon testifies that about a month after Edith's murder, Henry contacted her to tell her she'd better keep quiet "if she wanted to keep breathing." Since she had no memory then of being at the house, she understood him to be referring to what Edith had told her.

She says she's never had any mental problems. Nothing like this ever happened before. The police did not hypnotize her. She cannot explain why she did not help her friend that night nor why she blacked out for so long.

On cross-examination, Frizelle strikes at the accuracy of Gordon's account.

Q: You spent many hours with the police in the past few months, right?

A: Yes.

Q: They didn't believe you when you told them you weren't there, did they?

A: No.

Q: They kept telling you you were at the house, that you saw something you were not telling them, right?

A: Yes, they wanted the truth.

Q: And these interviews went on for hours and hours, didn't they?

A: Yes, a long time.

Q: They kept pressing you.

A: Well . . . yes . . .

Q: And you were tired and exhausted?

A: Yes.

Q: And they kept saying you were there, that you saw something, someone?

A: Yes.

Q: Until you finally broke down—

A: It's when I saw the deadbolt sticking out . . . it all just came back.

Q: And what came back was what the police told you, isn't that right?

A: Part of it, yes, but it was true just the same. I remember it now.

The prosecution rests. The defense calls its first witness, William Cordrey, a neighbor of the Barkers. At about 10:15 on the night of the murder he heard dogs barking and went out on his porch to see what was happening. He saw a large woman in Bermuda shorts running from the Barker residence. At almost the same time he saw a man with long hair walking fast in front of the house. He is quite sure from their size and weight that neither person was Henry or Edith Barker.

Defense counsel shows him a photograph.

Q: I ask you to look at this picture and tell us if the man and woman shown here are the same ones you saw that night.

He studies the photograph, holds it far away, then up close.

A: The guy had long hair like that. The lady was on the chubby side like this one. There's a resemblance all right. But I can't say positively. No way.

"Your Honor," defense counsel says, "the D.A. and I stipulate that this is a photograph of Jack and Jeannette Wister."

On cross-examination the D.A. shows Cordrey a photograph of Amy Gordon as she looked seven years ago. Cordrey says the woman in the photo also resembles the woman he saw that night in height and weight, but he can't be sure.

Sarah Frizelle calls Henry Barker. The tension heightens. You see him close up for the first time when he takes the stand. He makes a good appearance, but the anxiety shows in his face. He testifies he married Edith ten years ago in Norfolk, Virginia, when they were both in the navy. When they moved to San Diego, she left the navy and he reenlisted. A door-to-door salesman sold him the insurance policies, and he wasn't sure about the amounts until Ordway explained them. Then he wanted to change the benefits. He denies ever planning to kill Edith. He denies ever having any conversation with Jack Wister about killing Edith and says Wister has a bad reputation for honesty. He confirms Sally Lester's testimony as to the discovery of the body. He says Amy Gordon had it in for him because Edith told her he was having an affair with Sally, which wasn't true.

Mary Ward moves to the podium to begin her cross-examination. Her first questions focus on the life insurance.

Q: You now admit there was at least $30,000 insurance money on Edith's life?

A: Yes.

Q: Which you've already collected?

A: Yes.

Q: Do you remember the police asking you how much insurance there was on Edith?

A: I don't recall.

Q: I'll show you this police report. See if it refreshes your memory.

"May I approach, Your Honor?" Ward asks the judge.

"You may."

She goes to the witness stand with a document and shows it to Barker.

Q: Remember now?

Barker studies the paper.

A: I still don't remember.

Q: Do you dispute the conversation occurred?

A: I guess not.

Q: And did you tell the police, just a few days after the murder, the amount of insurance there was on Edith's life?

A: By looking at the report, I guess I did.

Q: And didn't you say, "$5,000, just enough to cover burial expenses." Didn't you say that?

A: According to the report, yes.

Q: And why didn't you tell the police the truth—that it was $30,000?

A: Because it didn't stick in my mind.

Q: Now, moving on, do you remember taking a navy cruise in the summer of 1976?

A: I do.

Q: And when you came back didn't something happen that made you very angry at Edith?

A: Not very angry, no.

Q: Upset?

A: Well . . . yes.

Q: Tell the jury what it was.

A: Well, she told me she'd had an affair with somebody else while I was at sea.

Q: And didn't that make you angry?

A: Well . . .

Q: Betrayed?

A: Sort of . . . yes.

Q: And didn't that make you want to get back at her, to hurt her for what she'd done to you?

A: No. We talked it over. We worked it out.

Q: Now, going to the night Edith was murdered, a phone call was received at your residence. Did you ever tell the police what it was?

A: No.

Q: Why not?

A: Because I had no recollection of it. It was a hectic time. I was very upset.

Q: Could it have been Leonard Keck asking if the police had gotten there yet?

A: No, he didn't even have our phone number. We had an unlisted phone.

"Nothing further."

Frizelle has a few questions now.

Q: Mr. Barker, at any time did you discuss with anyone a plan or intent or motive to kill Edith Barker?

A: No, I've never discussed killing anybody with anyone else.

Q: Did you participate in any way in the murder of Edith Barker?

A: No, definitely not.

Barker turns and looks directly at you with his deep blue eyes, "I swear I did not!"

Mary Ward stands up for one last shot.

Q: You admit you knew Leonard Keck?

A: Sure. Sally introduced us.

Q: Did you send him a note a few weeks before the murder?

A: Yes.

There is a noticeable pause. You notice the other jurors leaning forward.

Q: What did it say?

A: I asked him to get me some drugs . . . I was into drugs then.

Q: Did you send him some money after Edith's death?

A: I did.

Q: For what?

A: For the drugs he sent me.

Q: That's all?

A: That's all.

Q: It had nothing to do with the murder?

A: Nothing whatsoever.

———

Possible verdicts:
1. Guilty of first degree murder
2. Not guilty

WHAT IS YOUR VERDICT?

[Before choosing your verdict, see Jury Instructions 1–3, 5–10, 19, 20, starting on page 197.]

QUESTIONS AND ANALYSIS

Q1.   The police detained six persons as suspects for the murder of Edith Barker. Who were they, and why were they suspected?

Q2.   Why wasn't Leonard Keck ever called as a witness?

Q3.   Do you find credible Amy Gordon's testimony that she forgot her experience at the murder scene for six years and then suddenly remembered it?

Q4.   In the event the jury finds the defendant not guilty, would such a verdict mean the same as innocent?

———

A1, A2.   Who killed Edith Barker? Or assisted in killing her? Was it Henry Barker? The facts pointed to him as the one who hired Leonard Keck to do the job. He had the motives: revenge for Edith's infidelity, the insurance proceeds, and possibly a desire for Sally. But it was all circumstantial evidence, and the jury was instructed that if there are two reasonable interpretations of the evidence, one pointing to guilt and one pointing to innocence, then they must choose the interpretation pointing to innocence.

Leonard Keck? As the hit man, he was the primary suspect as the actual killer. Amy Gordon said he looked in every way like the man she saw, but she couldn't be positive. He was tried separately, and never appeared as a witness in the Barker trial because he asserted his constitutional right not to testify under the Fifth Amendment.

Was it Sally Lester? She arranged the meeting between Barker and Keck, knowing Keck was a hit man. She behaved suspiciously after discovering the body, and seemed uninterested in Edith's plight. She apparently had intercourse with Barker in her room. Was she in love with Barker? If so, she had the motive of wanting him for herself and moving into the master bedroom. In fact, she continued living in the house with Barker after the murder.

Ordway too had a possible motive: he received $15,000 from Barker, which he never repaid. Was that a payoff? He too acted suspiciously at the murder scene. He could not explain why he made no effort to revive Edith when he saw her unconscious, even though he was an expert in first aid.

What about Jack and Jeannette Wister? A man and woman observed at the scene matched their description. Jack had a criminal record, knew several hit men, used drugs, and admitted that when Barker asked him what it would cost to have Edith killed, he told him it would be five thousand dollars.

A3. Amy Gordon's loss of memory for six years may seem bizarre, but it can be explained psychologically. Forensic experts tell us an event can be so frightening or embarrassing or guilt-provoking that certain persons will block it out of their memory in order not to relive that terrible moment. Psychologists call this *psychogenic amnesia*, a phenomenon that is not uncommon. Suddenly a reminder may occur—in this case the sight of the deadbolt sticking out of the door—which can trigger the memory and bring it all back. The prosecution argued that this is precisely what happened to Amy Gordon. However, defense counsel had a different interpretation: that big gaps in her memory were filled in by suggestions of others—the police in particular—and her testimony was only a rendering of what she'd been told, even though she believed it really happened, a memory implanted by suggestion.

A4. See discussion under Verdict.

VERDICT

NOT GUILTY

Barker had two trials. The first resulted in a hung jury. In the second trial the jury acquitted him and set him free. The major hurdle for the prosecution was to overcome the jury's reluctance to accept Amy Gordon's story. It could not be done. Jurors said they had a strong suspicion of Barker's guilt, but the circumstantial evidence simply did not rise to proof beyond a reasonable doubt.

The jury's verdict illustrates a common misconception by the American public. The verdict of Not guilty does not mean the jury found Barker innocent. It only means he was not *proven* guilty beyond a reasonable doubt. We have no such verdict as Innocent in our criminal law.

What about Leonard Keck? He likewise had two trials, and likewise a hung jury in the first, acquittal in the second.

Who killed Edith Barker? After seven years of investigation and four jury trials, it is still a mystery.

LYNN DANIELS v.
ALAN KAUFMAN, M.D.

You are juror number twelve in a civil suit brought by a woman against her former lover for the intentional infliction of emotional distress. She seeks $1,000,000 in damages.

As they confer with their attorneys a few feet away from you, plaintiff Lynn Daniels and defendant Alan Kaufman remind you of warriors poised for combat. They seldom look at each other, but when they do they glare. She is an attractive woman, dressed in a tight-fitting designer suit. He is a good-looking man with horn-rimmed glasses and a receding hairline. You can understand how they were drawn to one another.

But in this scene she is huddling with her attorney, Dan Greenberg, at the table as the first witness is about to be called. She whispers to him with her lips almost touching his ear. Now Greenberg stands and says in a strong, authoritative voice: "We call the defendant, Dr. Alan Kaufman, as our first witness."

The doctor looks surprised. You hear him whisper to his defense attorney, "Can they do that?" The attorney, Lee Meisner, with gray hair and a weather-beaten face, merely nods in response.

The judge notices that some of the jurors appear taken aback by the plaintiff's maneuver. "You may not be aware," the judge says to the jury, "that in a civil case either side may call the opposing party as its witness and may cross-examine that witness. That is not true, of course, in a criminal case. There the defendant has a constitutional right to remain silent. No such right exists in a civil case.

"Dr. Kaufman may be sworn."

Dan Greenberg begins.

Q: What is your occupation?

A: I am a licensed physician, a psychiatrist.

Q: Do you have a subspecialty?

A: Yes. Sex therapy.

Q: You are an expert in that field?

A: I am.

Q: Where did you meet Lynn?

"Objection, Your Honor," defense attorney Lee Meisner says. "The use of first names is undignified."

"Sustained."

The doctor testifies he met Lynn Daniels through a personal ad. She had placed it—actually her mother had placed it—in the local newspaper ("Successful businesswoman seeks relationship with caring professional man.").

Q: Did you form an intimate relationship?

A: What do you mean, intimate?

Q: Of a sexual nature?

A: She wanted to the first time we went out, but I . . .

This time it is the questioner himself, Dan Greenberg, who protests: "Objection, Your Honor! Nonresponsive."

"Sustained. Just answer the question, Doctor."

The doctor testifies that he and Lynn Daniels did indeed become sexually involved. After a few months she moved into his six-bedroom townhouse. At his request she agreed to pay $2,000 a month toward the mortgage. After two pregnancies that resulted in miscarriages, the quarreling began in earnest.

Greenberg continues the questioning.

Q: Was she depressed over this second miscarriage?

A: Yes.

Q: She was crying?

A: Yes. We were sitting on the bed.

Q: What did she say?

A: She felt real bad. Her dreams of having a child hadn't come true.

Q: What did you do?

A: I tried to console her. But then I got tired of trying to be emotionally supportive to her. It seemed I was always doing that. I got up from the bed and walked away. I got hit in the back with the cordless phone.

Q: That made you angry?

A: It sure did. I went back to her, jumped on the bed, straddled her, and held her down. I told her to stop acting like a baby. I didn't hit her.

Q: Do you know why she threw the phone?

A: No.

Q: No idea?

A: No.

Q: Didn't you just say to her, "You killed the baby"?

A: Not in those words . . .

Q: Words to that effect?

A: Well . . .

Q: What words?

A: I said she'd done things to increase the possibility of miscarriage.

Q: Like what?

A: She wouldn't take the thyroid medication regularly.

Q: Medication that you as a doctor prescribed for her?

A: Yes.

Q: Did you accuse her of doing anything else to bring on the miscarriage?

A: Yes. That she was working too hard in her business.

Q: Working to pay the $2,000 a month you insisted she pay for the mortgage on your house?

A: We'd agreed to that.

Q: This all happened the day after the second miscarriage?

A: Yes.

Q: As a psychiatrist, do you think that was the proper way to react to her depression?

A: Well, I was tired of her acting like a child. She wouldn't do what she was told. I had to straighten her out.

Dr. Kaufman testifies that Ms. Daniels became pregnant a third time. This time she had the baby, a girl they named Chloe. He hired a Mexican housekeeper and governess, Filomena, to help with the baby. Ms. Daniels continued to travel in her business as a buyer and distributor of expensive women's designer clothes. She didn't trust Dr. Kaufman with the care of Chloe, so she usually had Chloe and Filomena travel with her. There was hope that having the baby would end the hostilities, but it didn't. When she returned from her business trips, she would accuse him of having affairs with other women.

Q: Was that true?

A: No.

Q: So did you decide to do something about her accusations?

A: Yes. I decided to teach her a lesson.

Q: How did you do that?

A: Well . . . I'm not proud of this—

Q: You mean the incident with the doll?

A: Yes.

Q: You placed a life-size blow-up doll in your bed?

A: Yeah.

Q: Describe the doll for the jury.

A: It was a sex toy. It's sold at adult stores, ostensibly for sex use.

Q: Where did you get it?

A: From a patient of mine. I insisted he turn it over to me because he had become overly obsessed with it to the point where he wasn't socializing with anyone else.

Q: Let me get this straight. This is a doll for performing simulated sex acts?

A: Right.

Q: And while Ms. Daniels was away you placed the doll in the bed you and Ms. Daniels slept in?

A: Just before she got home, yes. It wasn't very attractive . . .

Q: Oh?

A: It had yellow braids and blue eyes. It was flesh-colored.

Q: So where were you immediately before Ms. Daniels came in?

A: I got in bed.

Q: With the doll?

A: Yeah.

Q: What time of day was this?

A: About ten A.M.

Q: Did you call out to her after you heard her enter the house to let her know you were up there?

A: I'm fairly certain I did not.

Q: Did you put any clothing on it?

A: A pair of pantyhose. The legs were ugly.

Q: Isn't it a fact you tied pantyhose around the doll's neck?

A: No. It didn't have a neck.

Q: Didn't you do that as a threat of what could be in store for her?

A: No.

Q: Had you slept with the doll while Ms. Daniels was away?

A: I don't recall if I slept with the doll or not. I think I just put it in the bed when I heard her drive up.

Q: And then you got in bed with the doll?

A: Yeah. I was in bed with the doll when she came into the house, yeah.

Q: Tell this jury why you did this, Dr. Kaufman.

A: I'd become frustrated with her daily allegations that I was having sexual contacts with other women, none of the allegations being true. And it was probably poor judgment . . . in a stupid way . . . I decided that since she was so certain it was happening, I'd shock her a bit when she came back, so she'd think she'd actually caught me at something.

Q: Is this part of your sex therapy?

"Objection!" the defense attorney, Lee Meisner, says.

"Sustained."

Q: And how did she respond when she walked in?

A: She responded the way I thought she would: she screamed and yelled and didn't stop. She pulled the covers off, and acted frightened of the doll.

He testifies further that after this incident Ms. Daniels bought her own home, moved into it, and took Chloe and Filomena with her. She also invited Dr. Kaufman to move in with her, which he did after selling his townhouse. He admits he struck her physically once after that, but only to defend himself. He had picked her up at the airport and was driving her to his sister's house. Chloe, nearly two years old at the time, was in the backseat. His father had just arrived from St. Louis and was anxiously waiting to see the baby for the first time, his only grandchild. So they were all going to his sister's house for a family dinner. But Ms. Daniels didn't want to go. They argued. She grabbed the steering wheel to turn it in another direction. He stopped the car on the side of the highway to avoid an accident, and she began flailing at him. He fought back to ward off her blows. Chloe was sitting up, wide-eyed, watching everything.

Q: Did you grab her throat?

A: I just put my hands up to defend myself.

Q: Did you see the bruises on her throat afterward?

A: I saw one or two on the side of her neck, nothing great.

The fight on the highway in front of Chloe made him realize they had to separate. So he bought another house and moved out. Over the years they had bought several marriage licenses, but the licenses always expired. They had still never married. He denies he threatened to take Chloe away with him so that Lynn would never see her again. He denies he ever threatened to kill her in front of Chloe.

After he moved out the battle continued.

Q: You had hired the governess Filomena?

A: Yes, on the recommendation of friends who also had Mexican servants.

Q: Did you know if she was in the country legally or not?

A: I didn't know. I suspected she was illegal.

Q: But you went on paying her while you lived with Ms. Daniels?

A: Yes. Everyone else was doing it.

Q: And shortly after you moved out did you make a phone call to the Immigration and Naturalization Service in Miami, Florida, about Ms. Daniels and Filomena?

A: Yes.

Q: You were aware of Ms. Daniels's airline schedule for that trip, so you knew when she'd be landing in Miami with Filomena and Chloe?

A: Yes.

Q: What did you tell the INS?

A: I told them to watch for an illegal alien landing in Miami.

Q: And you gave them Ms. Daniels's name and said she was trying to smuggle an illegal alien into the state of Florida?

A: Yes.

Q: What did the INS say?

A: They thanked me for being a patriotic citizen.

Q: What did you say?

A: I said, "I try to do what I can."

The doctor denies the plaintiff's complaint that he stalked or followed her or her friends. He denies ever burglarizing her home after he moved out but admits friends offered to help him get his things from her house.

Q: Who were these friends?

A: Don't know.

Q: They called you on the phone?

A: Yeah, but I didn't recognize the voices. They said they would help me get my stuff, since there was no court restraining order on their going to the house like there was on me.

Q: And did you encourage them to go into her home?

A: I just listed what the items were that were mine, and that was it.

Q: And these items were later delivered to you?

A: To my house, yes.

Q: And you didn't see who delivered them?

A: No.

Q: And you have no idea who these strange voices were?

A: No.

Q: Moving to another point, did you ever threaten to kill Ms. Daniels?

A: Not really, no.

Q: What do you mean, "not really"?

A: Well, she's made life miserable for me with this lawsuit—lied in court about me—won't let me see Chloe. Sure, I've told people recently that I would like to see her dead.

Q: Who did you tell?

A: My attorneys—all members of my family—

Q: Ever say you'd consider killing her?

A: Yes. It's something I felt . . . But I'm not going to act on it. Feelings and thoughts are different from actions.

Q: So you've had homicidal thoughts about Lynn?

A: Yeah. That's a real common thing in psychiatry—homicidal ideation.

Q: Must be nice to analyze your own statements and their psychological ramifications.

"Objection!" Meisner says angrily. "Counsel is making a statement. That's not a question."

"Sustained. Jury will disregard counsel's last statement."

Q: Thank you, Your Honor. Dr. Kaufman, did you say to someone in your office recently who was worried about you, "I am not going to kill myself. I might kill Lynn, but not myself"?

A: That's just what I said, yeah.

The doctor is excused and steps down from the stand. As he passes the plaintiff's table you notice him whisper something to her under his breath, but you cannot make it out.

The next witness for the plaintiff is Anthony Pacelli of the United States Border Patrol in Miami, Florida. He testifies he received a call from a gentleman who said he wanted to give the government a hot tip.

Q: Did he give you his name?

A: No, sir. He said he wished to remain anonymous.

Q: What did he say?

A: He said a female named Lynn Daniels would be arriving on an American Airlines flight—he had the number—that evening with an illegal alien she was trying to smuggle into Florida. He said there'd be a baby with them, too.

Q: What action did you take?

A: My partner and I went to the airport and spotted them when they got off the plane.

Q: And did you detain them?

A: Oh, yes sir. The lady—Ms. Daniels—was very upset. She had to go to some meetings. But the Mexican lady didn't have papers—she was illegal all right.

Q: So you held them for questioning in a detention room?

A: Yes, sir. The American lady—Ms. Daniels—broke down. She was crying uncontrollably . . . sobbing . . . very distressed. She said she thought the nanny was legal. After several hours we let Ms. Daniels go with the baby. But the nanny—we had to hold her.

Q: After you found out the whole story, do you think you'd have detained Ms. Daniels if you knew the facts?

A: I doubt it, sir. But of course we have to do our job.

Defense attorney Meisner cross-examines.

Q: Officer Pacelli, you say Ms. Daniels was crying uncontrollably?

A: Yes, sir.

Q: She ever tell you she had acting lessons and won awards for acting?

"Objection!"

"Sustained."

Now at last the star and catalyst of this proceeding, Lynn Daniels, is called to the witness stand. She testifies how she met Alan Kaufman, how her mother put the ad in the paper without her even knowing about it, and how he was one of about ten men—doctors and lawyers mostly—who answered, how she felt immediately attracted to him. He told her he owned a 5,000-square-foot home with three acres, two cars, and a boat. She knew her mother would be extremely pleased if she were to marry a doctor. He certainly had all the things that made a successful doctor in her eyes. She was thirty years old at the time and had an income of over $100,000 a year in her business as a buyer, but what she really wanted was a good husband and child. The career was not important to her. When they moved in together he demanded she pay $2,000 a month toward the mortgage, and she didn't protest.

Near tears, she tells of the night after her second miscarriage.

A: He kept telling me it was my fault for being on my feet so much. He kept yelling at me that I had killed the baby and said I never wanted the baby . . .

Q: Did you throw the phone at him?

A: I had the phone in my hand. I'd picked it up to call my mother to ask her to come get me . . . I threw the phone down . . . He grabbed me, threw me up against the wall . . . I remember going down . . . He was on top of me, straddling me . . . He started to choke me . . . both hands . . . for a minute he put pressure with his hands on my neck, hard enough to leave bruises, visible . . .

She gives a different version of the fight in the car. He picked her and Chloe up at the airport and told her he'd made plans for dinner with his father at his sister's house. He wanted to take Chloe without her.

"I said, 'I'll go too. I don't want you taking Chloe without me.' "

Q: Why didn't you want him to take Chloe without you?

A: Because he'd never taken care of her alone, and I wasn't sure he could.

Q: What did he do?

A: He pulled over and cut the engine. Chloe was sitting up in the back car seat.

Q: What did he say?

A: He said: "You —, don't you ever tell me what I can and can't do."

Q: Did he strike you then?

A: He tried to strangle me. He held his hands around my throat. I started screaming for the police and he said, "You'll be dead before the police ever get here."

She points to the right side of her neck to show the jury where the bruises were.

A: He had his thumbs right here, cutting off my windpipe. He held his hands like that for two minutes until I hit his arm and broke his grasp.

Q: What was Chloe doing?

A: She was screaming. He said, "Don't you tell me I can't take Chloe whenever I want," and he grabbed my hair and pulled my head into the gearshift. It didn't break my nose, but it was bleeding.

Q: What happened after that?

A: We went to dinner with his father. I cleaned up as best I could, and I don't think they noticed anything. When we were driving home after dinner I told him to get the hell out or I was going to the police. He said if I went to the police he would kill me.

She says the defendant testified truthfully about the doll incident except for one thing: the doll had pantyhose tied around its neck, which she understood to be a threat of what could happen to her.

For several months she kept telling him to leave, but he wouldn't do it. "He said he would take Chloe with him, and I'd never see her again. He said, 'I'm not leaving until I'm good and ready, and you can't make me, and if you do, I'll make your life hell.' "

Finally, she says, she obtained a court order forcing him to leave. Then came the arrest in Miami. The Border Patrol agents told her she was being detained for smuggling an illegal alien across state lines. They took her into a little room and kept her there with Chloe and Filomena. She was not mistreated, but it was a degrading experience. After several hours they let her go with Chloe but kept Filomena. She had to find a bail bondsman to post bail for Filomena. The agent told her she'd been set up.

Ms. Daniels calculates she lost over $60,000 in sales and commissions because of the delay. She missed several meetings and lost two major accounts at a time critical to her business. During her detention she was unable to phone buyers to notify them.

Upon her return to San Francisco she discovered her home had been burglarized. Liquor, toys, and gifts to Chloe were missing. The police told her that entry had been made by someone with a key, and since Dr. Kaufman was the only other person with a key, she suspected him, especially when she found his photograph faceup on the bedroom floor—his signature to the burglary. As a result she had all the locks changed, installed a new security system, and even hired a guard to watch the house when she had to be away. The cost was $6,500.

This time she obtained a court order restraining him from coming within 100 yards of the house, but she still saw him driving by at strange hours. Sometimes when friends left her home she'd see him following them. Once she got a call from her friend Alma Dawson, who said, "Alan's following me. What shall I do?" She'd look out the window and he'd be sitting outside in his car. She called the police; he was gone when they came, but he would come back when they were gone.

The defense attorney, Meisner, cross-examines.

Q: With regard to the argument in the car on the highway, you say you had bruises on your neck afterward?

A: Yes.

Q: You're making this up, aren't you?

A: No. I am not making it up.

Q: Ms. Daniels, isn't it true you were bulimic at the time?

Greenberg jumps up. "Objection! Irrelevant! He's trying to embarrass the witness."

"Your Honor," Meisner says, "if the court please, I will show it is very relevant to her claim that my client tried to strangle her."

Judge: I will allow it subject to a motion to strike.

A: Yes, I was bulimic.

Q: Which means you would make yourself throw up from time to time?

A: Yes. It's a terrible sickness, really.

Q: And to do that you would stick your fingers down your throat?

A: Yes.

Q: Show us how you would place your fingers.

Greenberg starts to object. "Your Honor—"

"Do I have to, Your Honor?" Daniels asks as she turns to the judge. "It's very . . ."

"All right," Meisner says, "I'll do it myself. I'll demonstrate." He stands up, places two fingers in his mouth. "Is this the way?"

A: The fingers have to go in more.

Q: Like this?

A: Farther.

Q: Like this?

The fingers go in a bit farther.

A: Farther, farther.

You can hear the sarcasm in her voice.

The judge is grinning. Meisner removes his fingers. His thumb is pressed against his throat. He has a look of triumph as he shows the jury the position of his thumb.

Q: And didn't you always place your thumb against your throat like this?

A: No.

Q: And isn't this exactly how you got those bruises on your throat?

A: No, Mr. Meisner, that's not how at all.

The plaintiff rests.

Meisner opens the defense case for Dr. Kaufman by calling a number of witnesses as to the doctor's character. Several members of his family testify that he has always had a reputation as a nonviolent, law-abiding citizen. His father and sister testify they were present at the dinner after the alleged strangling in the car. They sat close to Ms. Daniels and saw no bruises on her neck of any kind. She was wearing a white suit, and they did not see any blood spots on it such as might drip from a nosebleed.

The defense also calls a private investigator, Jason Holloway, who testifies he was hired by the court to supervise the visits by Dr. Kaufman to see Chloe. The parties would arrive in separate cars at a prearranged spot in a parking lot. Ms. Daniels would bring Chloe. The investigator would park in the middle between them and stand by to keep the peace. He would bring the baby to Dr. Kaufman, where the doctor would hold the baby for thirty minutes, after which the baby would be returned to its mother and all parties would leave. Dr. Kaufman would always appear affectionate and caring during such visits.

Q: Did you ever hear her make any threats to him at these visits?

A: Yes, sir. I heard her say she'd sue him unless he promised to stay away from Chloe.

As the witness steps down you notice Dr. Kaufman whispering to his attorney, who promptly announces he will call the doctor back to the stand.

Q: Doctor Kaufman, I want to ask you about these homicidal thoughts you had—

A: Yes, sir. That's all they were, just thoughts.

Q: You never intended to act on them?

A: Absolutely not.

Q: Tell me this: what's the highest level of education you've attained?

A: I've had three years of specialty residence in psychiatry following my M.D. degree.

Q: How did you do in high school?

A: I was top in my class.

Q: And how did you do in college?

A: I graduated magna cum laude with honors in two majors.

Q: And you've been a practicing psychiatrist now for twelve years?

A: Yes.

Q: And you've also been in analysis yourself?

A: Yes, sir. As part of the training.

Q: Now then, considering all your education and experience, do you feel you are especially aware of your thoughts, your thought processes?

A: Oh, yes. More so than the average person. I make a strong distinction between thoughts and actions. They are two separate things.

When Dr. Kaufman leaves the stand for the last time, Meisner looks over at Daniels. He stares at her for a second, then says, "I call Lynn

Daniels back for further cross-examination.

"Ms. Daniels, you are reminded you are still under oath."

A: Thank you, Mr. Meisner.

Q: Now tell us, what makes you think you've suffered severe emotional distress?

A: I have nightmares. I'm choking in my sleep. I feel Alan's hands around my throat.

Q: This still going on?

A: Oh, yes. I wake up screaming and crying.

Q: Well, tell me this; have you ever gone to a psychiatrist for the treatment of the emotional distress which you say my client inflicted on you?

A: No, sir.

Q: Never gone to a professional for help?

A: No, sir.

Q: Well, if you're really suffering so much, why not?

A: You really want to know?

Q: Yes—or is it simply that it's not been serious enough to bother? She takes a deep breath.

A: You really want to know?

Q: Yes.

A: Alan's a psychiatrist. Somehow I don't trust them at the moment.

QUESTIONS AND ANALYSIS

[Before answering the following questions, see Jury Instructions 2, 21–23, starting on page 197.]

Lynn Daniels seeks a total of $1,000,000 in damages. The judge instructs you to state your finding of liability and award of damages, if any, as to each allegation separately. You may include both compensatory damages (actual out-of-pocket losses) and punitive damages (punishment for despicable conduct). In the second column of the verdict form you are to answer yes or no to the question of liability. If your answer is yes, list the amount of your award in the third column.

Question	Yes or No	Award
1. Did Defendant place in Plaintiff's bed a life-size doll with a stocking tied around its neck with the intent to shock her?	_____	$_____
2. Did Defendant try to strangle Plaintiff in front of their minor child and tell Plaintiff he would kill her?	_____	$_____
3. At another time did Defendant tell Plaintiff he would kill her?	_____	$_____

Question	Yes or No	Award
4. Did Defendant tell Plaintiff he would take Chloe away and that Plaintiff would never see her again?	_____	$_____
5. Did Defendant contact Immigration and Naturalization Service in Miami and cause Plaintiff to be detained for smuggling aliens?	_____	$_____
6. Did Plaintiff suffer a loss in her business as a result of Defendant's conduct?	_____	$_____
7. Did Defendant burglarize or cause someone to burglarize Plaintiff's home?	_____	$_____
8. Did Defendant so terrify Plaintiff by his burglary that she was required to install a security system?	_____	$_____
9. Did Defendant stalk, follow, and monitor actions of Plaintiff and her friends?	_____	$_____
10. Did Defendant push Plaintiff's face into the gearshift of her car, causing her nose to bleed?	_____	$_____

The tort of Intentional Infliction of Emotional Distress is still relatively new in American history. For a long time courts were reluctant to allow damages for emotional distress unless it was accompanied by physical injury. Not until the second half of the twentieth century did the doctrine become fully accepted. Peace of mind is now recognized as a legally protected interest.

The decision by the plaintiff's attorney to call the defendant as the first witness was a smart tactic. Inexperienced plaintiff's attorneys often miss the opportunity to score early in the trial by calling the defendant and other opposing witnesses in the plaintiff's case-in-chief.

Here is the jury's verdict as to each allegation.

VERDICT

Question	Yes or No	Award
1. Did Defendant place in Plaintiff's bed a life-size doll with a stocking tied around its neck with the intent to shock her?	Yes	$ 25,000
2. Did Defendant try to strangle Plaintiff in front of their minor child and tell Plaintiff he would kill her?	Yes	$ 75,000
3. At another time did Defendant tell Plaintiff he would kill her?	Yes	$ 28,000
4. Did Defendant tell Plaintiff he would take Chloe away and that Plaintiff would never see her again?	Yes	$ 25,000
5. Did Defendant contact Immigration and Naturalization Service in Miami and cause Plaintiff to be detained for smuggling aliens?	Yes	$256,250
6. Did Plaintiff suffer a loss in her business as a result of Defendant's conduct?	Yes	$160,000

Question	Yes or No	Award
7. Did Defendant burglarize or cause someone to burglarize Plaintiff's home?	Yes	$ 50,000
8. Did Defendant so terrify Plaintiff by his burglary that she was required to install a security system?	Yes	$ 25,750
9. Did Defendant stalk, follow, and monitor actions of Plaintiff and her friends?	Yes	$ 25,000
10. Did Defendant push Plaintiff's face into the gearshift of her car, causing her nose to bleed?	No	$ −0−
TOTAL:		$670,000

The fact that the defendant was a psychiatrist, who should have known better, was certainly a factor in the jury's award.

JURY INSTRUCTIONS

Jury instructions comprise the law of the case being tried. Most jury trials involve numerous written instructions—too numerous to include here—which are submitted by counsel, approved by the judge, read by the judge to the jury, and often submitted to the jurors for their reference while deliberating.

1.
DUTIES OF JUDGE AND JURY
(Criminal Cases)

Whether a defendant is to be found guilty or not guilty depends upon both the facts and the law.

As jurors you have two duties to perform. One duty is to determine the facts of the case from the evidence received in this trial and not from any other source. Your other duty is to apply the rules of law that I state to you to the facts as you determine them and in this way to arrive at your verdict. It is the judge's duty to explain to you the rules of law that apply to this case. You must accept and follow the rules of law as I state them to you.

As jurors you must not be influenced by pity for a defendant or by prejudice against him or her. You must not be biased against the defendant because he or she has been arrested for this offense or because he or she has been charged with a crime, or because he or she has been brought to trial. None of these circumstances is evidence of guilt, and you must not infer or assume from any or all of them that the defendant is more likely to be guilty than not guilty.

You must not be swayed by mere sentiment, conjecture, sympathy, passion, prejudice, public opinion, or public feeling. Both the state and the defendant have a right to expect that you will conscientiously consider and weigh the evidence and apply the law of the case, and that you will reach a just verdict regardless of what the consequences of such verdict may be.

2.
NOT ALL INSTRUCTIONS APPLY

The following instructions apply to the rules of law that may be necessary for you to reach verdicts in the trials presented. Not all instructions apply to each case. Whether an instruction applies will depend on the nature of the charge and your determination of the facts.

3.
BURDEN OF PROOF
(Criminal Cases)

A defendant in a criminal case is presumed to be innocent until the contrary is proved, and in case of a reasonable doubt whether his or her guilt is satisfactorily shown, he or she is entitled to a verdict of not guilty. This presumption places upon the state the burden of proving him or her guilty beyond a reasonable doubt. The defendant has no burden of proof.

Reasonable doubt is defined as follows: It is not a mere possible doubt, because everything relating to human affairs, and depending on moral evidence, is open to some possible or imaginary doubt. It is that state of the case which, after the entire comparison and consideration of all the evidence, leaves the minds of the jurors in that condition that they cannot say they feel an abiding conviction, to a moral certainty, of the truth of the charge.

4.
RIGHT TO REMAIN SILENT

It is a constitutional right of a defendant in a criminal trial that he or she may not be compelled to testify. You must not draw any inference from the fact that he or she does not testify. Further, you must neither discuss this matter nor permit it to enter your deliberations in any way.

5.
DIRECT AND CIRCUMSTANTIAL EVIDENCE

Evidence is either direct or circumstantial. Direct evidence is evidence that directly proves a fact without the necessity of an inference.

Circumstantial evidence is evidence that proves a fact from which an inference of the existence of another fact may be drawn.

It is not necessary that facts be proved by direct evidence. They may be proved also by circumstantial evidence or by a combination of direct and circumstantial evidence. Both direct evidence and circumstantial evidence are acceptable as a means of proof. Neither is entitled to any greater weight than the other.

However, in any case based on circumstantial evidence, if the circumstantial evidence is susceptible of two reasonable interpretations, one of which points to the defendant's guilt and the other interpretation to his or her innocence, you must adopt that interpretation which points to the defendant's innocence and reject that interpretation which points to the defendant's guilt.

If one interpretation appears reasonable and the other interpretation appears unreasonable, you must accept the reasonable interpretation and reject the unreasonable.

6.
MURDER

Murder is the unlawful killing of a human being with malice afore-thought.

7.
MALICE AFORETHOUGHT

"Malice" means either an expressed intent to kill or an intent to commit an act dangerous to human life with knowledge of the danger to, and with conscious disregard for, human life.

"Aforethought" means the malice must precede the act.

8.
FIRST DEGREE MURDER

First degree murder occurs when the killing is committed with malice aforethought and a deliberate and premeditated intent to kill.

9.
DELIBERATE AND PREMEDITATED

"Deliberate" means determined after careful thought and weighing of the consequences. "Premeditated" means considered beforehand.

The law does not try to measure in units of time the length of time during which the thought must be pondered before it can ripen into an intent to kill that is truly deliberate and premeditated. The time will vary with different individuals and different circumstances.

The true test is not the duration of time but the extent of the reflection. A cold, calculated decision may be arrived at in a short time, but a mere unconsidered rash impulse will not amount to deliberation and premeditation, even though it includes an intent to kill.

10.
LESSER OFFENSES IN HOMICIDE CASES

If you are not satisifed beyond a reasonable doubt that the defendant is guilty of first degree murder, he may be found guilty of any lesser offense, i.e., second degree murder, voluntary manslaughter, or involuntary manslaughter—if the evidence is sufficient to establish his guilt of such lesser offense beyond a reasonable doubt.

(In the case of *State* v. *Sarko* only, an additional possible lesser offense is Aiding or Encouraging a Suicide.)

11.
SECOND DEGREE MURDER

Second degree murder occurs when the killing is with malice aforethought but without deliberation and premeditation.

(*Note:* There are other forms of first and second degree murder, but they do not apply to the cases presented.)

12.
VOLUNTARY MANSLAUGHTER

Voluntary manslaughter is the intentional killing of a human being without malice aforethought.

An intentional killing is said to be without malice aforethought and therefore reduced to voluntary manslaughter in the following circumstances:

1. Where the killing is committed during a sudden quarrel or heat of passion; and where the provocation is such that it would naturally arouse such passions; and where the killer acts under the smart of that heat of passion.

The heat of passion that will reduce a murder to manslaughter must be such as naturally would be aroused in the mind of an ordinary reasonable person in the same circumstances.

2. Where the killing is committed in the honest but unreasonable belief in the need to defend against imminent peril to life or great bodily injury.

13.
INVOLUNTARY MANSLAUGHTER

Involuntary manslaughter is the unlawful killing of a human being without malice aforethought and without an intent to kill. This crime is committed when the killing occurs as a result of an act of gross negligence involving a high risk of death or great bodily harm.

14.
DIMINISHED MENTAL CAPACITY

If the defendant's mental capacity was reduced by mental illness or intoxication or any other cause, you may consider its effect on the defendant's ability to form the mental states of the intent to kill or malice aforethought.

You may not find the defendant guilty of first degree murder if, because of his or her diminished mental capacity, you have a reasonable doubt as to whether he or she did maturely and meaningfully deliberate and premeditate upon the gravity of the act.

Further, you may not find the defendant guilty of either first or second degree murder if, because of a diminished mental capacity, you have a reasonable doubt the defendant could form the mental state of malice aforethought.

Thus, a finding of diminished mental capacity can reduce a first degree murder to second degree murder, and a second degree murder to voluntary manslaughter as outlined above.

(*Note:* Among the cases in this book, the law of diminished capacity applies only to the case of *State* v. *Schaeffer,* since the doctrine was abolished by the state legislature after that case.)

15.
RIGHT OF SELF-DEFENSE

The killing of another person in self-defense is justifiable and therefore not unlawful when the person who does the killing honestly and reasonably believes:

1. That there is imminent danger that the other person will kill him or her or cause him or her great bodily injury, and

2. That it was necessary under the circumstances to kill the other person to prevent death or great bodily injury to himself or herself. "Imminent" means the danger must be immediate.

16.
ACCIDENT

When a person commits an act by accident under circumstances that show no evil purpose, intention, or culpable negligence, he does not thereby commit a crime, and he must be found not guilty.

17.
KIDNAPPING

Every person who unlawfully and with physical force moves any other person against her will and without her consent for a substantial distance is guilty of kidnapping.

18.
ATTEMPTED RAPE

The crime of attempted rape as charged against the defendant in *State* v. *Buckles* is an attempted act of sexual intercourse with a female person not the wife of the perpetrator, without her consent.

An attempt to commit rape consists of two elements, namely, a specific intent to commit rape, and a direct but ineffectual act toward its commission.

19.
PRINCIPALS

The persons concerned in the commission of a crime who are regarded by law as principals in the crime and equally guilty thereof include:

1. Those who directly and actively commit the act constituting the crime, or
2. Those who aid and abet the commission of the crime.

20.
AIDING AND ABETTING DEFINED

A person aids and abets the commission of a crime when he or she intentionally aids, promotes, or encourages the commission of the crime with knowledge of the unlawful purpose of the perpetrator.

21.
DUTIES OF JUDGE AND JURY
(Civil Cases)

It is my duty to instruct you in the law that applies to this case.

It is your duty to follow the law. As jurors it is your duty to determine the effect and value of the evidence and to decide all questions of fact.

You must not be influenced by sympathy, prejudice, or passion.

22.
BURDEN OF PROOF
(Civil Cases)

The plaintiff has the burden of proving by a preponderance of the evidence all of the facts necessary to establish the allegations in the complaint.

"Preponderance of the evidence" means evidence that has more convincing force than that opposed to it.

23.
INTENTIONAL INFLICTION OF EMOTIONAL DISTRESS

The charge of intentional infliction of emotional distress requires proof by a preponderance of the evidence that the defendant engaged in outrageous conduct with the intent to inflict emotional distress and that the plaintiff suffered severe emotional distress as a result.